2000 MORE INSULTS

2000 More Insults

Compiled by Louis A. Safian

THE CITADEL PRESS   Secaucus, N.J.

Fourth paperbound printing

Copyright © 1967 by Citadel Press, Inc.
Published by Citadel Press
A division of Lyle Stuart, Inc.
120 Enterprise Ave., Secaucus, N.J.
In Canada: George J. McLeod Limited
73 Bathurst St., Toronto, Ont.
Manufactured in the United States of America
ISBN 0-8065-0521-4

Contents

Introduction	7
Bamboozlers	11
Birthdaze	17
Boozers	20
Chatterboxes	26
Cranks	30
Cream Puffs	34
Do-Nothings	37
Dressed and Undressed	41
Dumbbells	45
Entertainers	58
Egotists	62
Failures	67
Fallen Angels	72
Features	76
Figures	83
Flat Tires	91
Goat-Getters	95
Gold Diggers	100
Gossips	105
Husbands	109

Hypochondriacs	118
Juvenile Delinquents	121
Liars	123
Losers	127
Lowbrows	130
Meanies	133
Muddleheads	135
Nudists	137
Perfect Pairs	139
Playboys	141
Playgirls	149
Political Acrobats	156
Screwballs	158
Show-oafs	160
Snobs	163
Tightwads	165
Wet blankets	168
Wives	171
Writers	182
Nicknames	184
Squelches	189

Introduction

Like its predecessor, *2000 Insults for All Occasions*, this volume is a compilation of capsule caricatures, rapid-fire repartee and roguish ribs for all those who can view human shortcomings, vagaries, and pretensions with a keen sense of humor.

The comic insult is far from being of contemporary origin. It has always been in vogue in this funny and strange world full of funny and strange people doing funny and strange things for funny and strange reasons. From ancient times it has been in high favor with knowing wits for sizzling squelches and on-the-spot ammunition to dissolve deserving targets in acid retorts.

Said the French philosopher and satirist Voltaire, "You can't tell the truth without singeing someone's beard." Flattery itself might well be defined as insult wrapped as a gift. As soft soap (90 per cent of which is lye), it plays upon a person's vanity and susceptibility with its insincere excessiveness of praise. Inversely, the so-called insult gag has the virtue of calling a spade a spade. It offers everyone with a perceptive eye and a sensitive recording ear a comical but nonetheless commonsensical view of people's characteristics, actions, speech, and peculiarities of dress and appearance.

As in *2000 Insults for All Occasions*, I have sprinkled the pages of this book generously with virtually every form of sardonic wit and humor. The alert reader will recognize such specimens as paradoxes, comic similes, puns, reversible meanings, hyperboles, spoonerisms, boners, ironies, and firecracker repartee, and to seize upon many of them for his own nefarious use in conversation, speech, and writing.

As with the earlier volume, this sequel is designed to put the right retort in the right head at the right time. It is tailor-made for those who observe human foibles with ironical amusement, and who only need a handy thesaurus of bons mots, wisecracks, and pot shots for the fullest expression of their critical faculties.

Human nature being what it is, the insult gag is most popular when it is directed at someone else, since no one other than its hapless target ever identifies himself with it. Used, however, good-humoredly and without malice, to characterize mankind's failings collectively, it is certain to be most effective as a well-enjoyed laugh-getter. It can also be used in reverse for rewarding effect by the simple expedient of switching from the third-person personal pronoun to the first.

It is to be hoped that this compilation will enjoy its predecessor's gratifying popularity as a handy "goadbook," and as a laugh-package of rib-tickling reading.

LOUIS A. SAFIAN

2000 MORE INSULTS

Bamboozlers

His mind is a real scheme engine.

He gets along fine; he's living off the fatheads of the land.

It's been so long since he's been upright, his shadow is crooked.

He's always up and doing—up to trickery and doing everybody.

His friends don't know what to give him for Christmas. What do you give a guy who's had everybody?

He'll go down in history as the leading exponent of the age of chiselry.

He belongs in Hollywood as a character actor. When he shows any character, he's acting.

If he offers you a deal, see your lawyer—and if your lawyer approves, see another lawyer.

You're safer trusting a rabbit to deliver a leaf of lettuce than to trust him.

He's so crooked, he can hide in the shadow of a corkscrew.

He's so crooked, when he dies they'll have to screw him into the ground.

Help him when he's in trouble, and he'll never forget you—especially the next time he's in trouble.

He never worries ahead of time. He's sure he can always double-cross a bridge when he comes to it.

When he's in a department store, the clerks all shake his hand —to keep it out of the cash register.

He comes from a family of writers. His brother writes novels, his sister writes songs, his mother writes poetry. He writes bum checks.

He's very superstitious. In a fight, he always keeps a horseshoe in his glove.

He never lets a day go by without doing someone good.

He's managing his life on the cafeteria plan—self-service only.

Don't take his checks if you're allergic to the smell of burning rubber.

He not only wants to eat his cake—he also wishes for some other fellow's cookie.

He's hoping for a lucky stroke—his rich uncle's.

With him as your financial adviser, you can run your fortune into a shoestring.

He's the kind of guy who can take it or leave it—mostly he takes it.

When he borrows money, it's not only against his principle to pay interest, but also against his interest to pay the principal.

He's willing to do an honest day's work—only he wants a week's pay for it.

He has a sure-fire method for saving money. He forgets whom he borrowed it from.

He has always paid his taxes with a smile—the Internal Revenue Service is now after him for the cash.

It may be that all the people can't be fooled all the time, but he sure is trying.

In his present job as treasurer, it's been found that he banked five times his salary in two years. The company is investigating— to see what took him so long.

When you lend him money, he's telling the truth when he says, "I'll be everlastingly indebted to you."

He never puts off till tomorrow what he can put over today.

It doesn't take long to notice that his character is like a decayed walnut—it's not what it's cracked up to be.

He's so two-faced, he stands up in both the top and bottom halves of the seventh inning of a ball game.

He pretends to be burying the hatchet when he's only digging up the dirt.

The way he discharges an obligation, you can hear the report miles away.

He's sure to leave pussyfoot prints on the sands of time.

The only time he isn't himself is on Sundays in church.

A wealthy widow has been paying his expenses on a vacation in Paris—he's a real Paris-ite.

He's the type who'll sell himself to the highest biddy.

He fell in love with a woman at second sight. The first time he saw her he didn't know she was rich.

He denies that he married her because her dad left her a fortune. He insists he would have married her no matter who left it to her.

He's the type who can soft-soap you so that you can't see for the suds.

His flattery makes you feel like a pancake that's just had the syrup poured on it.

He's one of those professional reformers who manage to get the pie out of piety.

At a dinner party, he's the guy who's sure to eat all the celery.

He can convince you that you're going places when he's really taking you.

He's a guy that's really going far—always one step ahead of his creditors.

Lend him money and you'll learn the difference between capital and labor. The money you lend him represents capital—getting it back represents labor.

His success is the result of two things—luck and pluck. Luck in finding someone to pluck.

He's a real success story. He started out with $1,000; now he owes $100,000.

He's so crooked, he has to screw his socks on.

He's so sneaky, he could steal second base with his foot on first.

He's the most highly suspected person in the community.

He's one of those self-effacing, sweet, unpresuming persons—a real phony.

If all the breath he expends on his phony claims could be converted into power, it would supplant atomic energy.

He's a first-class kibitzer—always willing to bet your shirt on someone else's hand.

He claims he does his duty as he sees it—boy, does he need an optometrist!

To get 10 per cent out of him, you've got to be at least his 50-50 partner.

In his footprints on the sands of time he'll leave only the heel marks.

He doesn't do as well at bowling or at the races as he does at poker. That's because he can't shuffle an alley or keep a horse up his sleeve.

He always has a lot of trouble with those fluffy, thick hotel towels—he can hardly close his suitcase.

His wallet is always full of big bills—all unpaid.

He claimed a tax exemption for his mother who's been dead five years. His explanation: "Mother's still very much alive in my heart."

He's making a good living selling burial suits with two pair of pants to people who believe in the hereafter.

He can sell a double-breasted suit to a chap with a Phi Beta Kappa key.

He not only gets a girl up to his apartment to see his etchings, he even sells her a few of them.

Once he hit a man and knocked him six feet in the air; then he sued him for leaving the scene of the accident.

Looking at the high prices on the restaurant menu, he says to his date, "What'll you have, my plump doll?"

When he slaps you on the back. it's only to make sure that you'll swallow what he's told you.

He's making money bottling ashes from a crematorium and selling them to cannibals as Instant People.

You wouldn't even put it past him to pin badges on frankfurters and sell them as police dogs.

He spends a lot of time shining up to the boss instead of polishing off some work.

He not only expects to get something for nothing; he also wants it gift-wrapped.

He recently advertised: "Man with income tax blank would like to meet lady with income."

He has more crust than a pie factory.

He's just a little boy, after all—after all he can get.

If he ever fell over his own bluff, that would really be his downfall!

He's always dating his checks ahead. If he should die, say, on May 15, his tombstone inscription will undoubtedly read: He Died May 15th, as of June 1st.

Birthdaze

She claims she's just turned thirty—it must have been a U turn.

Her youth has changed from the present tense to pretense.

She says she's just reached 32. Everyone is curious to know what detained her.

You really can't raise an eyebrow when she says she's only 29. Anybody who sticks to the same story for ten years has to be telling the truth.

She never really lies about her age. She simply says she's as old as her husband—and then she lies about his age.

She's 42, going on indefinitely.

She claims she's approaching 35. Everybody wonders from which direction.

No more candles for her on her birthday cake. On her last birthday the candles looked like a prairie fire.

Now that she's reached 40, it's like launching a rocket—she's started her countdown.

Once on the witness stand she was instructed by a gallant judge: "Madam, state your age—then take the oath to tell the truth."

If you ask her her age, she tells you it's her business—and she's been in business quite a long time.

She claims that she feels like a young colt, but she looks more like an old 45.

She'll never live to be 50. Not at the rate she's been overstaying at 40.

She's a very decisive person. By the time she reached 45, she had definitely decided what she wanted to be—36.

You can tell her age like you do a used car's. The paint job may conceal the age, but the lines show the years.

She claims that when she was eighteen the President of the United States gave her a beauty prize. It's hard to believe that Woodrow Wilson had time for that silly stuff.

There's a woman who really knows how to keep her age—as a matter of fact, she hasn't changed it in seven years.

She says she's around 30, and in a way she's right—nearly the second time around.

The only thing she'll admit about her age is that she's pushing 40. She's not pushing it—she's dragging it.

She's not lying when she claims she just turned 23—she's 32.

On her last birthday she baked the cake herself and inserted the candles—one for every year. She had every reason to be prouder of the design than of her arithmetic.

On her last birthday there were enough candles in the cake to give everyone there a suntan.

The guests tried to count the candles on her cake, but the heat drove them back.

You can't call her a "fast woman." Although 35, she hasn't reached 29 yet.

She was born in the year God only knows when.

It's not that she's shy or demure when she doesn't tell her right age—she dishonestly can't remember.

She's so old, she can get winded at a run in her stockings.

She knew Madame Butterfly when she was a caterpillar.

Boozers

He's not one to do things in halves—he does them in fifths.

When he returns from lunch, he's so loaded they make him use the freight elevator.

The way he's drinking, liquor mortis is sure to set in.

One of these days he'll be killed by a flask of lightning.

He's been frequenting a new night club. It has the nicest tables he's ever been under.

In college he had the reputation for being the highest student in the class, and was voted the man most likely to dissolve.

It's not true that he does nothing but drink—he also hiccups.

He has his doctor worried—he has too little blood in his alcohol stream.

So far as he's concerned. "Sweet Adeline" is the Bottle Hymn of the Republic.

The skeleton in his closet is in the shape of a whiskey bottle.

When he gets a cold, he buys a bottle of whiskey, and in no time it's gone. Not the cold—the whiskey.

There's been a marked difference in his drinking since he's been going to a psychiatrist. Now he drinks on the couch.

There's hardly a morning when he doesn't get up with a toot-ache.

Once he went to a party incognito—stone sober.

He's the nicest chap on two feet, if he could only stay there.

In taverns all over town he's regarded as one of their unsteadiest customers.

He's been expelled from Alcoholics Anonymous. He wasn't anonymous enough to suit them.

The cocktails on his expense account run into a staggering figure.

He's a very friendly drinker. He's always shaking hands—even when no one else is around.

He's been hiccupping a lot lately—just messages from departed spirits.

He gets very indignant when told that he drinks too much—particularly when he can't stand up to dispute it.

An orthopedist is immobilizing his elbow. He drinks so much, everytime he bends it, his mouth snaps open.

If it wasn't for the pretzels, he'd be entirely on a liquid diet.

He can sit for hours in a tavern, where he pays as he glows.

He spends so much time in bars, he's developing rheumatism from picking up wet change.

A woman drove him to drink. He's remembering her in his will as an expression of his gratitude.

He has never cultivated the fine art of nixing drinks.

He frequents so many bars, his suits aren't dry-cleaned—they're distilled.

He's been drinking Bloody Marys mixed with carrot juice. They haven't sobered him any, but he sees better.

If there's a nip in the air, he even tries to drink that.

An entomologist would be interested in him—he's a rare specimen of a barfly.

When you say he's "soused," you can mean it in the "full" sense of the word.

The only thing his health means to him is something to drink to.

He's a man with a lot of liquid assets.

He's having his elbows furrowed so they won't slip off wet bars.

The only exercise he ever gets is hiccupping.

On his last birthday, with just one breath he lit all the candles on his birthday cake.

When the boss asks him to work overtime, he demands time and a fifth.

They have an apt name for him—Jack the Pint Killer.

He's half Scotch—and half shot most of the time.

In a saloon his conversation always buds in the nip.

He's been warned that liquor is a slow poison, but he says he doesn't mind—he's in no hurry.

He's a very public-spirited individual—he always drinks spirits in public.

It takes only one drink to make him drunk, but he's not sure whether it's the ninth or the tenth.

There are times he gets so lit up you can read by him during a blackout.

At the rate he consumes liquor, you can hear the pretzels splash as he eats them.

No wonder they call him "Truck"—he always has a load on.

He's an alcoholic intellectual—a fried egghead.

He's been unsteadily employed at the same job for the past ten years.

He believes in a balanced diet—a highball in each hand.

He's handsome after a fashion—after a couple of old-fashioneds.

At a party he never plays Spin-the-Bottle. He won't let go of it.

At bedtime he drinks a pint of whiskey for his bad case of insomnia. He hasn't cured it, but it's making it a pleasure to stay awake.

Bartenders all over town warn him not to stand up while the room is in motion.

He's a man of settled habits—he's settled down to a continuous round of drinking.

He's a kiss-and-tell, tippling lover. All his loves are brandied about.

Several times he's been held up on his way home; in fact, it's the only way he could have gotten home.

You have to take his drinks apart to see what makes him hic.

Once, in the hospital, he kept asking for water, and everyone knew without a doubt that he was delirious.

His eyes and nose are so red, the Communist Party has sent him a membership card.

He deducts his liquor bills as a medical expense. His customers and he always drink to each other's health.

He's an outstanding candidate for the Alcohol of Fame.

The way liquor makes him fly, bartenders are asking him to land some other place.

A judge told him: "It's alcohol, and alcohol alone, that's responsible for your condition." He answered: "You've made me very happy, judge. Everyone else tells me it's all my fault."

He's been getting so high, he'll have to drink soon with a net under him.

He'd go on the wagon anytime—if he could find one with a bar.

He sure knows how to carry his liquor. When he opens a bottle he gets carried away.

He often goes on a crying jag when he's in a state of melancholism.

He was recently a judge in a beauty contest. The competition wasn't very stiff—but he was.

When he donates blood to the Red Cross, there's so much alcohol in it, they use it to sterilize the instruments.

He's playing a better round of golf lately. He can go around now in a little less than a quart and a half.

He enjoys an energizing workout when he gets up, so he has his own parallel bars—one for rye and one for bourbon.

The way he's flying blind, he'd better sober up real soon for a landing.

The distance between his office and his favorite bar is four blocks going and five blocks coming. He walks straighter going than coming.

It's called for a tremendous amount of will power on his part, but he's finally succeeded in giving up trying to give up drinking.

He's been on the new Drinking Man's Diet, and now he's a thin lush.

He's been using a bourbon-flavored toothpaste. It hasn't helped cut down on his cavities, but "Who cares?" he says.

Recently he fell downstairs with a quart of whiskey, but he didn't spill a drop—he kept his mouth shut.

He's one guy that wasn't just born—he was mixed!

It isn't the *ein* or the *zwei*, but the *drei* martini that gets him lit.

He drinks to soothe and steady his nerves. The trouble is he gets so steady he can't even move.

He hates the very sight of liquor. That's why he drinks so much—to get it out of sight quickly.

He's been practicing yoga as a cure. It hasn't exactly cured him, but now he can get soused standing on his head too.

He talks with more claret than clarity.

It's his ambition to join the Diplomatic Corps. If he ever gets there, he'll live on protocol, alcohol, and Geritol.

He'll never get married. His girl won't marry him when he's stewed, and he won't marry her when he's sober.

Chatterboxes

She's a constant source of earitation.

He's a great talker—one of the best you can ever hope to escape from.

She has a voice that's very hard to extinguish over the telephone.

She can talk 50 per cent faster than anyone can listen.

When she talks you can't even get in a word sledgewise.

He's the type that holds everyone spielbound.

Why, it even takes him two hours to tell you that he's a man of few words.

The smaller his ideas, the more words he uses to express them.

It's not accurate to say that she always has the last word— she never gets to it.

She has a very disconsolate parrot. He's never had a chance.

There are any number of things in life that go without saying —her tongue more than anything else.

She must have been raised on tongue sandwiches.

Her husband can bend a horseshoe with his bare hands, but she can tie up twenty miles of telephone wire with her chin.

He has a picture of her that he took with a highspeed camera —her mouth was closed for a split-second.

It's easy to understand why she talks twice as much as most women—she has a double chin.

She even talks to herself—to be sure of getting in the last word.

Her mouth is so big, it takes her fifteen minutes to get her lipstick on.

She could even have the last word with an echo.

His idea of an ideal conversation is one part you and nine parts me.

He's had ten sets of dentures. He doesn't lose them—he wears them out as a nonstop talker.

You get a gliberal education listening to him.

You like him a lot when you first meet him, but he soon talks you out of it.

No one is his equal at using more words to say less about nothing.

It's just too much to hope that one day he may come forth with a few brilliant flashes of silence.

His lodge brothers are far safer taking their fingers out of a dike than letting him take the floor at a meeting.

He regards free speech not as a right but as a continuous obligation.

He has never made a mistake—and for a good reason. He's never stopped talking long enough to do anything.

He's bought a dozen books on "How to Speak in Public." What he really needs is one on how to shut up.

He thinks by the inch and talks by the yard, until you feel like removing him by the foot.

They call him "the Westerner," because he comes into a room shooting from the lip.

He's a specialist in monopologues.

He makes you wish you were wearing a hearing aid so you could shut him off.

She has a gift for conversation, and everybody would be happy to give her another one to stop talking.

She's the type who's always babbling over with enthusiasm.

It's simply amazing how—with only one tongue and two eyes—she can say more than she sees.

Where she's concerned, one word leads to another 10,000.

You can count on her to respond to any wordy cause.

She's just returned from the seashore with a sunburned tongue.

With her, you can't think twice before you speak—not if you want to get a word in.

She claims that she travels to broaden her mind, but it only seems to lengthen her conversation.

With operations too common these days to talk about, she's hoping for a real serious one so that she can work it into a conversation.

She's the kind of woman who would be enormously improved by laryngitis.

She's sure to be an old maid. She'll never quit talking long enough for any man to kiss her.

Her feelings get terribly hurt when you talk while she's interrupting.

He's as gabby as a barber.

On the witness stand, she swore to tell the truth and the whole truth—but not to stop there.

She's like a clothes moth—always chewing the rag.

He says the Constitution of the United States permits him to talk as much as he likes. The trouble is, the United States has a stronger constitution than his listeners.

His father was an auctioneer and his mother was a woman— thus he comes by his talkativeness naturally.

You can be sure of one thing. He wouldn't listen to you talk if he didn't know it was his turn next.

He regards even a minute's pause in conversation as a social indiscretion. It's his signal to go right back into verbal high gear.

As a conversationalist he's inimitable—and illimitable.

He always has too much conversation left over at the end of his ideas.

He can speak for an hour without a note—and without a point.

His expenditure of words is too great for his income of ideas.

He says the only trouble with his speaking is that he doesn't know what to do with his hands. He should hold them over his mouth.

As a speaker and conversationalist he reminds you of that famous Chinese philosopher, *On Too Long*.

On the golf course his trap is more annoying than any of the others on the course.

No wonder he's always leading with his chin—his mouth is wide open.

Cranks

One thing an alarm clock never arouses is his better nature.

He has such a long face, barbers charge him double for shaving it.

The idea for whiskey sours must have come from a look at his face.

He's a chip off the old glacier.

He doesn't get ulcers—he gives them.

He has a perfect way of ending office conferences. He says: "All those opposed to my plan say 'I resign.'"

He arrives at the office promptly at 9:00 A.M. in a huff, and departs in it at 5:00 P.M.

There are so many yes men working for him, his firm is called "the Land of Nod."

When he finishes dining, waiters always ask him, "Sir, was anything all right?"

He should have been an undertaker—he has no use for anyone living.

He can cut you dead faster than a coroner performing an autopsy.

One time he was sick in bed for a week, and his secretary sent a sympathy card to his wife.

The last time he was in a hospital, he got get-well cards from all the nurses.

He's always willing to face the music—so long as he can call the tune.

He can become very unpleasant once you get to NO him.

Someone should tell him to idle his motor when he feels like stripping his gears.

He likes people who arrive at firm convictions—after they know what *he* thinks.

His liver is out of order, and his opinions are the same.

The thing he finds hardest to give is in.

His new glasses have helped his vision without changing his prejudiced point of view.

It would be interesting to know on what he biases his opinions.

He really should see a psychiatrist about his infuriating complex.

He hates know-it-alls—those who insist he's wrong.

His favorite expression is: "My mind is already made up, so don't confuse me with the facts."

There are times when he smiles when things go wrong—he has just thought of someone he can blame it on.

His one-track mind wouldn't be so bad if he was ever on the right track.

It's as easy to convince him as to get the hump off a camel's back.

He's so opinionated, his wife said to him one Sunday, "Tomorrow will be Monday, *if it's all right with you*."

To him life is a mirror and he's always looking for a crack in it.

He's very quick on the flaw.

If he ever gets to heaven, he'll tell the angels, "I don't believe in the heretofore."

As a first-nighter at the theatre, he's always ready to stone the first cast.

He looks for faults as if they were buried treasure.

Give him something for free, and he'll gripe that it wasn't gift-wrapped.

He can make more cutting remarks than a surgeon.

Everything looks yellow to his jaundiced eye.

He hasn't been himself lately. Everyone hopes he'll stay that way.

He got where he is by the sweat of his browbeating.

Someone should tell him it takes only 15 facial muscles to smile and 65 facial muscles to frown, so he should stop overworking himself.

He's as glum as a tongue-tied parrot.

You can always depend on him to contribute more heat than light to a discussion.

His staff meetings are called "listening-things-over sessions"—nobody else expresses an opinion.

He writes all his office memos on "rapping" paper.

The only time he's pleasant is when his staff puts in a good week's work in a day.

You can't help admiring him if you work for him. If you don't, you're fired.

The bone of contention in most of his arguments is above his ears.

There may be some rare moment during the day when he isn't disgruntled, but he's certainly far from being gruntled.

What a loser he is! He may be gripping the winner's hand, but he's glaring at his throat.

When he praises you, it's like having the hangman praise your pretty throat.

He'd better keep his words soft and sweet—one of these days he may have to eat them.

He wins all his arguments—but no friends.

He has a chip on his shoulder. It's easy to understand—there's wood higher up.

Cream puffs

He never has to worry about his station in life. Everyone is always telling him where to get off.

They have an apt nickname for him—Old Man Quiver.

When a fight starts, he always does his best—100 yards in 10 seconds.

He got into an argument once and could have licked his opponent with one hand—only he couldn't get him to fight with one hand.

He's as jumpy and fidgety as a long-tailed cat in a room full of rocking chairs.

He's more nervous than a turkey in November.

At the first sign of trouble, he thinks with his legs.

He's such a lightweight, he could tap-dance on a chocolate éclair.

If he goes into an auto showroom just to use the phone, he buys a new car because he hasn't the nerve to walk out without buying something.

He even says "Thank you" when an automatic door opens for him.

He has a sure-fire way of handling temptation—he yields to it.

He's a man of firm convictions. It manifests itself as soon as he knows what anyone else thinks on a given subject.

When he goes to a dentist, he needs an anesthetic just to sit in the waiting room.

Late TV horror pictures don't scare him. When they're over, he just crawls out from under his chair and makes a beeline for his bed.

On his way from home to the airport he even buys insurance for the limousine ride.

He bites his nails so much, his stomach needs a manicure.

He'd commit suicide if he could do it without killing himself.

He's the type of person who can make coffee nervous.

In his spinal column, all the bone is in a lump at the top.

They call him "the Caterpillar"—he keeps his job only by crawling.

You can break him easier than a biscuit.

He's always burying his head in the sand like an ostrich—that's why he's such a tempting target.

He crumbles up like an old ruin under responsibility.

His motto is: "It isn't who you know but who you yes."

His big trouble is that he never NO's his own mind.

He's the kind of guy who falls for everything and stands for nothing.

When faced with danger and threatening disaster, he sets his teeth, assesses the situation in the twinkling of an eye—and then runs faster than a jack rabbit who hears the howl of a wolf.

Since playing the stock market, he's stopped riding in elevators. He can't stand hearing the operator say, "Going down, going down!"

He has such a low, inferior opinion of himself, he wouldn't join any organization that would take him in as a member.

Maybe he doesn't exactly retreat in a fight, but he sure manages to back up enough for a good running start.

He's thankful that he lives in a free country where a man could say what he thinks, if he wasn't afraid of his wife, his boss, and his neighbors.

He'll never get over the embarrassment of having been born in bed with a woman.

She's so nervous she can thread the needle of a sewing machine while the machine is running.

She's never been the same since she opened the refrigerator and saw a Russian dressing.

He wouldn't say boo to a goose.

He's the sort of namby-pamby who gets lost in a crowd of two.

He's as spineless as spaghetti.

He's a willing minion to mass opinion.

In any emergency, he's as helpless as the owner of a sick goldfish.

It's not true that he kisses his boss's feet every day. His boss doesn't come to the office every day.

He has overcome his fear of flying. Pretty soon he may be fearless enough to open his eyes and watch the movies.

He's the kind of mollycoddle who asks permission to ask permission.

The only time he ever walks around with his head high and erect is when he has a stiff neck.

In a recent fight he had his opponent really worried. The guy thought he had killed him.

The average number of times he says "no" to temptation is once weakly.

Do-nothings

He's well known as a miracle worker—it's a miracle when he works.

You can tell he isn't afraid of work. Look at the way he fights it.

As a youngster, he swallowed a teaspoon and hasn't stirred since.

His boss is giving him a raise. His snoring keeps the rest of the employees awake.

He's so lazy, he sticks his nose outside, so the wind can blow it.

There's only one job he's interested in—as a tester in a mattress factory.

He's so lazy his feet hurt before he gets out of bed.

He's taking trombone lessons because it's the only instrument on which you can get anywhere by letting things slide.

His prayers are printed and pasted on the wall. At bedtime, he points to them and says, "Lord, please read them."

He's a real steady worker. If he gets any steadier, he'll be motionless.

Money doesn't grow on trees—even if it did he wouldn't shake a limb to get it.

There's one thing you can say for him. He puts in a good day's work—in a week.

He works eight hours and sleeps eight hours. His boss is firing him because they're the same eight hours.

His boss said to him recently, "I'd like to compliment you on your work—*when are you going to start?*"

He has a standard excuse for loafing. He says, "A body is a machine, and I'm no mechanic."

Generous Nature has provided him with a big cushion to sit around on.

Doctors have diagnosed his case as one of lazyosis, in an advanced stage of idleingytis, with acute symptoms of workophobia, and fearemia of activity.

Asked whether he has any romantic notions, his wife says sadly, "Maybe he has notions, but no motions."

His boss and his wife are demanding to see his birth certificate for proof that he's alive.

His wife is buying him an appropriate gift—something timely and striking—an alarm clock.

The only reason he gets up from bed in the morning is because he can't carry it with him during the day.

He has found a great way to start the day. He goes back to bed.

He's so lazy he won't even exercise discretion.

It's too much of an effort for him to make coffee, so he puts coffee beans in his mustache and sips hot water.

He gets his exercise watching TV horror movies and letting his flesh creep.

During an earthquake alert, he sat up waiting for the shock to shake down his folding bed.

He stands with a cocktail shaker in his hand, waiting for an earthquake.

It's lucky for him that beer cans have been made easier to open —until then he didn't have any exercise at all.

To give you an idea of how lazy he is, he wouldn't even help move his mother-in-law out of his house.

He's one person not likely to walk through a screen door—he's too careful not to strain himself.

He can fall asleep even while running for a bus.

He's made a career out of collecting unemployment insurance.

He's known as the N.Y.U. man—New York Unemployed.

Talk about occupational hazards! He had a narrow escape—he was offered a job when he reported to pick up his unemployment check.

Asked once, "What did you do for a living?" he replied, "I don't know. I've been out of work so long, I forget."

Advised to get a job, invest his salary, and accumulate capital so in time he wouldn't have to work anymore, he replied, "Why do I have to go through all that? I'm not working now."

He's one of those clock-eyed individuals who can't see opportunities.

He's suffering from overwork—overworking his alibi for why he isn't working.

The only exercise he gets is pulling balky ice trays from the refrigerator.

When he got married he proudly told his wife—a successful career woman—that marriage and a career don't mix. Since then he's never worked.

He's a person with his feet definitely on the ground—the trouble is, he doesn't keep them moving.

He joins as many unions as he can, so as to be sure he'll be frequently out on strike.

December is the only month of the year when he works his fingers to the bonus.

Dressed and undressed

She dresses like a lady—Lady Godiva.

She shows a lot of style, and the style shows a lot of woman.

The only thing holding up her dress is a city ordinance.

She wears such tight dresses, the fellows in her office can hardly breathe.

That's a very cute dress she almost has on.

She wears clothes not only to look slim, but to make men look 'round.

Don't try to judge her by her clothes—there isn't enough evidence.

She calls her latest purchase a "going away" dress. It looks like the best part of it left long ago.

When complimented on a dress she wears, she says modestly, "Oh, it's really nothing!" How true.

Tight clothes don't stop her circulation. The tighter her clothes, the more she circulates.

If a moth ever got into her gown, it would die of starvation.

She's switched her style—from off-the-shoulder blouses to off-the-body gowns.

With that dress, it's hard to tell whether she's trying to catch a man or a cold.

A doctor went crazy trying to vaccinate her in a place where it wouldn't show.

She dreamed that she was strolling down the street with nothing on but a hat, and she was terribly embarrassed. It was last year's hat.

Her neckline is pretty near where her waistline ought to be.

She never has to worry about getting into a strip poker game —she has practically nothing to lose.

That dress of hers should be called Opportunity—there's lots of room at the top.

There's one sure reaction to her clothes—low and behold!

It isn't easy to tell whether her dress has a low neckline or a high hem.

She's excited about her new low-cut dress—in fact, she can hardly contain herself.

She wears her clothes so tight, she must like to squeeze out the last ounce of value.

She's a gal with a lot of hidden talent—and she wears clothes that reveal it.

Her slacks are so tight that if she had a coin in her pocket, anyone could tell if it's heads or tails.

She wouldn't be wearing slacks if she had as much hindsight as foresight.

It looks as if her stretch pants had been put on her with a spray gun.

It can truly be said that she wears those low-cut gowns for ample reasons.

She goes out wearing less than her mother wore in bed.

Just as she's given up hope of getting a perfect fitting dress, she luckily finds one that's two sizes too small.

At the year-end, all her friends wish her a Happy Nude Year.

She's one gal who gets along with the bare necessities of life.

Her friends are urging her to run for office, as the only candidate with nothing to hide.

With that strapless gown, it's obvious she's not interested in shouldering any responsibility.

She's very partial to one of her dresses. She wears it when she wants to look halfway decent—but not completely.

Her clothes go to extremes—never to extremities.

As she was leaving the house for a party, she suddenly decided she didn't feel like going, so she put on something and went to bed.

She doesn't find it difficult to meet men—she exposes herself in the right places.

When her friends saw her in that topless bathing suit, it was quite a letdown.

The last night club she went to had a minimum—she was wearing it.

She wears gowns that bring out the bust in her.

One of these days she'll have an accident—catching her foot in her neckline.

She wears sweaters to accentuate the positive, and girdles to eliminate the negative.

Nobody can squeeze more out of a bikini than she can.

She once read the saying, "Man wants but little here below." Maybe that's why her dresses are getting shorter and shorter.

She claims that her new dress is the latest model from Paris. That's not a model—it's a terrible example.

She's worn that dress so many years, it's been in style five times.

Her hat is becoming—becoming worn-out.

She wears a hat with delirium trimmins.

Nobody asks her to remove her hat at a movie—it's funnier than the movie.

With those clothes she wears, her friends have dubbed her "Mrs. Rummage Sale of 1960."

That dress she's wearing will never go out of style—it will look just as ridiculous year after year.

Dumbbells

She has a pretty little head. For a head, it's pretty little.

No one can accuse him of being scatterbrained. He hasn't any brains to scatter.

He has a strange growth on his neck—his head.

She's so dumb, mind readers only charge her half-price.

He's recovering from an unusual accident—a thought recently struck him.

Everyone is rooting for him to get ahead. They don't like the one he has.

She's like yesterday's coffee—a little weak in the bean.

Wisdom often comes with age, but with him age came alone.

He's undoubtedly older than he looks. He never could have gotten so fatheaded so quickly.

No one can drive him out of his mind. At most it would be only a putt.

Any time he gets an idea into his head, he has the whole thing in a nutshell.

He has a chip on his shoulder. It's a splinter from the wood above it.

He says he has a mind of his own. He's welcome to it. Who else would want it?

They call her "Plymouth Rock." She has a shape like a Plymouth and a head like a rock.

He has one of those mighty minds—mighty empty.

He's the world's greatest proof of reincarnation. Nobody could get that dumb in just one lifetime.

An intelligent thought dies quickly in his head—it can't stand solitary confinement.

He should study to be a bone specialist. He has the head for it.

He's always putting off decisions—he's waiting for a brainy day.

They're inventing a new kind of coffin that fits right over the head. It's for guys like him—dead from the neck up.

There's a good reason why he always has that stupid grin on his face—he's stupid.

He even wrinkles his brow while reading the comics.

They put better heads than his on umbrellas.

She has a soft heart, and she's let it go to her head.

He has a one-track mind, and the traffic on it is very light.

It's a waste of time to ask him "You know what?" Of course he doesn't.

She doesn't know her own mind—and she hasn't missed much at that.

You can't help feeling sorry for that poor little mind—all alone in that great big head.

It's stretching the imagination a lot to picture him as the end product of millions of years of evolution.

Many doctors have examined his head—but they can't find anything.

The only way she can make up her mind is to powder her forehead.

An idea recently went through his head. That's not surprising —there was nothing there to stop it.

A book has just been written about him—*How to Be Happy Though Stupid.*

He keeps his head when everyone about him is losing his. No wonder—he's just too dumb to understand the situation.

He can safely go into wild country inhabited by head-hunters. They'd have no interest in his.

He's one guy that must have a sixth sense. There's no evidence of the other five.

If it wasn't for the changes in weather, she'd never be able to start a conversation.

She's like Venus de Milo—beautiful, but not all there.

He must be even smarter than Einstein was. Twelve people were said to have understood Einstein. *Him* nobody understands.

If your doctor suggests that you exercise with dumbbells, ask him to join you for a walk.

His train of thought is just a string of empties.

All his life he's worked his head to the bone.

She has a skin of ivory—and so is her head.

He paid $500 to have his family tree searched, and found he was the sap.

Every once in awhile she stops to think; then she forgets to start again.

She has a baby face—and a brain to match.

Be careful how you exchange ideas with him. The result is sure to be a blank for your mind.

They've named a Chinese restaurant after him—Low I. Queue.

In life's battle for success, he doesn't have a secret weapon—like a head.

He was in a fight once, and was knocked conscious.

There are times when he does have something on his mind—he wears a hat occasionally.

He should be careful not to let his mind wander. It's too weak to be allowed out alone.

When he was promoted from the fifth to the sixth grade, he was so thrilled he could hardly shave without cutting himself

In school he got 100 in the exams—25 in Geography, 25 in Science, 25 in Arithmetic, and 25 in History.

Everyone called him "Corn" in school, because he was always at the foot of the class.

His parents always signed his report card with an X, so the teacher wouldn't know that anyone who could read and write had a son like that.

If ignorance is really bliss, he's the world's happiest guy.

He was born April second—one day too late.

The average man has 12 million brain cells; 11 million 990 thousand of his are unemployed.

If you traded on the stock market with his brains, you'd be wiped out fast.

The most underdeveloped territory in the world has just been discovered—it's under his hat.

His neck reminds you of a typewriter—Underwood.

If he ever talked about what he understood, the silence would be unbearable.

He'll never be too old to learn new ways to be stupid.

He's so dumb, he waters his garden with whiskey to grow stewed tomatoes.

He's hard at work on an invention—color radio.

He's crossing a piece of lead with a rabbit to get a repeating pencil.

He's feeding his hens racing forms so they can lay odds.

He's developing a new health food made of yeast and shoe polish. It's for people who want to rise and shine.

He's crossing a cow with a mule so he can get milk with a kick in it.

He's crossing asparagus with mustard to get hot tips at the racetracks.

He's working on a new invention—a bridge that goes halfway across a river, then turns and comes back again—for people who change their minds.

The only time he thinks is in a poolroom, where he can rack his brains.

He guards against being chilled to the bone—he always wears a hat.

He's not just an ordinary moron—he's the morons' moron.

Everything you say to her goes in one ear and out the other. There's nothing to block traffic.

It would take a surgical operation to get an idea into his head.

He should exercise his head more—to work off some of the fat between his ears.

The story of his life could be titled: *A Sap's Fables.*

Judging by the old saying "what you don't know won't hurt you," he's practically invulnerable.

He has to stand on his head to turn things over in his mind.

He could easily lose ten pounds of surplus fat—if they cut off his head.

He's getting a B.A. degree. He's finally mastered the first two letters of the alphabet—and backwards at that.

He's halfway between a low-grade intellect and high-class numskullery.

He's in real trouble. The electronic brain in the office broke down—now the boss expects him to think.

If you want to get the real dope about anything, go to the real dope—HIM.

He parts his hair in the middle because his head isn't well balanced.

He won't buy a concrete swimming pool. He says he doesn't like to swim in concrete.

He heard about a movie in which a hunter shot an elephant in his pajamas. He says it's silly—what would an elephant be doing in pajamas?

A traffic court judge asked him, "Have you ever been up before me?" He said, "I don't know, judge. What time do you get up?"

A lifeguard told him, "I've just resuscitated your daughter." He roared, "Then, by God, you'll marry her!"

Asked if any big men had ever been born in his town, he replied, "No, only little babies."

He's applying for an insurance policy so that if he should bump his head, they'll pay him a lump sum.

Told by an insurance agent that his company paid over $5 million for broken arms and legs, he asked, "What do they do with all of them?"

He bought a topless bathing suit for his half sister.

Once he saw an old woman fall down, but didn't pick her up. His mother had warned him not to have anything to do with fallen women.

When the librarian asked him if he wanted a heavy book or a light one, he answered, "It doesn't matter—I have my car outside."

He bought a million 1960 calendars for one cent apiece. He figures if 1960 ever comes back again, he'll make a fortune.

He had to see his doctor in the morning for a blood test, so he stayed up all night studying for it.

He shot his wife while buying a house, because the contract read: "Execute all three copies together with your wife."

He admits he's unfamiliar with the works of Sigmund Freud, but says he knows his brother, French.

He's never bought Christmas seals; says he wouldn't know what to feed them.

She was invited to a bridal shower, so she brought the soap.

Asked what she thought about the Common Market, she answered, "I really wouldn't know—my cook does all the shopping."

Following a honeymoon trip to the Twin Cities she had twins. On a later visit to Three Rivers, Ontario, she had triplets. Now she refuses to go with her husband to the Thousand Islands.

He stopped a guy from beating his donkey—a real case of brotherly love.

She won't go to a beauty parlor for a fingerwave. She says, "Who wants wavy fingers?"

She often serves her guests in the nude—whenever the cookbook says "Serve without dressing."

After reading *Les Misérables*, he still can't figure out which of the characters was "Les."

When she goes to a meeting, she never accepts tickets for a door prize. She says she has no use for a door.

A life insurance agent asked him, "Do you want a straight life?" He answered, "Well, I'd like to step out and fool around once in awhile."

The boss told her if her work didn't improve she'd find a pink slip in her envelope. She said, "How nice! Make it a size 36."

He made love to his wife in a jeep over a bumpy road so they'd have a bouncing baby.

He carried a double-barreled gun to the ball game because he heard the Lions were playing the Tigers.

He was asked for a contribution to help the Old Ladies' Home. His question was: "What are the old ladies doing out on a night like this?"

She yanked her daughter out of the co-ed school when she learned that boys and girls matriculated together and were required to engage in extracurricular activities.

She was horrified when her daughter returned from college saying that she weighed 118 pounds stripped for gym. "Who in blazes is Jim?" she wanted to know.

Tell him that since you last saw him a lot of water has gone under the bridge, and he'll be sure to ask, "What bridge?"

He's afraid to take his boots off for fear he'll hurt his feet when he kicks the bucket.

She keeps her baby in a high crib on an uncarpeted floor, so she can hear him if he falls out.

She lies in the sun for hours at the beach so she can be the toast of the town.

She was asked if she cared for Dickens, Shakespeare, and Keats, and she whispered, "Please keep your voice down; my husband has a terribly jealous disposition."

She was asked if she liked codfish balls. "I don't know," she said, "I never went to one."

He went to an oculist to have a tooth pulled. He knew it was an eye tooth.

He bought his girl a pair of stockings with a run in each one; he wanted to get a run for his money.

In the last election, voters were urged to vote bright and early. He voted early.

A real estate man asked him, "How would you like to see a model home?" He answered, "Swell! What time does she quit work?"

His doctor tells him that exercise will kill germs. He says it's silly—how can you get germs to exercise?

He didn't go to the movies to see *Dr. Jekyll and Mr. Hyde.* He doesn't like double-features.

A doctor told her she had acute appendicitis and she snapped indignantly, "Look, Doc, I came here to be examined, not flattered."

He's the kind of lunkhead who would buy the sleeping pills concession in a Niagara Falls hotel.

Where an employment questionnaire requested "Length of residence in home town," his answer was: "About 40 feet."

Asked whether she was in the arms of Morpheus last night, she answered indignantly, "I don't even know the man."

He denies the charge that he's illiterate. He says he can prove his parents were married.

There's no point in telling him a joke with a double meaning. He won't get either one of them.

He always begins a mystery novel in the middle, so he won't only have to wonder how it will end, but also how it began.

Peeking through a hole in the fence of a nudist colony, he was asked, "Are there men or women in there?" He said, "I dunno—none of them's got any clothes on."

He jumped off a bus backward when he heard a man say, "Let's grab his seat when he gets off."

About to extract his tooth, the dentist told the wife, "I'm giving him an anesthetic so he won't know anything." She said, "Don't bother—he doesn't know anything now."

She told her boss, "I'm fed up with the way you criticize my steno work. How do you spell 'quit'?"

Asked, after a late snack in a fellow's apartment, "Now, how about a little demitasse?" she snapped, "I should have known there was a string attached to the invitation."

As a plump tourist in Italy, she was curious to know what makes the Tower of Pisa lean, so she could take some too.

Her husband's name is Otto, and she still can't spell it backwards.

Statistics always confuse him. He heard that every minute a woman gives birth to a baby, and he thinks she should be stopped.

He read that a man gets hit by an automobile every twenty minutes. He says, "What a glutton for punishment that guy is!"

He called it quits when his fourth child was born, because he read that every fifth child born in the world is Chinese.

He wants to live to be 103. He figures he'll have it made then, because few people die after that age.

He took his daughter out of college when he learned that graduates of women's colleges have 1.8 babies.

He heard that more people die in bed than anywhere else, so he doesn't sleep in a bed.

He says if it hadn't been for Thomas Edison we'd all be watching TV by candlelight.

He's too scared to get married. Every time he's about to, some insurance man asks him to take out life insurance.

Asked whether he knows Poe's Raven, he replied, "No, what's he mad about?"

She can't find a thing to buy in antique shops. She claims they're not making antiques nowadays like they used to.

He won't let his daughter go to college because he heard that female students have to show their male professors their thesis.

The first time he heard about the Boston Tea Party, he asked who the caterer was.

He went to a fortuneteller to find out where he was going to die, so he can stay away from the place.

She's only had her present job for four days, and already she's two weeks behind in her work.

A fellow asked her if she was a somnambulist. She didn't know what it meant, so she slapped him just to be on the safe side.

He goes to a fortuneteller who charges $10 to read brilliant minds, and $5 for average minds. For him it's only 50 cents.

He keeps jumping up and down after taking his medicine— he forgets to shake the bottle.

She wonders why everyone thinks she has a crazy cat—they keep telling her she has a silly puss.

When a beggar asked him, "Can you give me a quarter for a sandwich?" he said, "Let's see the sandwich."

She came to the office in a bathing suit because the boss had promised to let her get in the office pool.

Sick as he was, he didn't go into the doctor's office because the sign read "9 to 1," and he wanted better odds than that.

He lost his dog, but he won't put an ad in the paper. He says it's no use—his dog can't read.

He was told to try nude painting as a hobby—now he's caught a cold.

She was ruined before she discovered that what her doctor had ordered was not—as she misunderstood—three hearty males a day.

Worried about her poor reflexes, her doctor asked her, "Do you ever wake up with a jerk?" She replied, "I'll have you know I'm pretty choosy about my boyfriends!"

He still hasn't bought an electric toothbrush. He doesn't know if his teeth are AC or DC.

Asked "How do you like bathing beauties?" he answered, "I don't know. I never bathed any."

When the new mayor announced that he was getting rid of some unnecessary bureaus, she wrote him that she was furnishing a new apartment, and could use some of them.

You can't trip him up. Asked to spell Mississippi, he'll come right back and ask whether you mean the river or the state.

He's never slept with his wife. He says it isn't honorable to sleep with a married woman.

She asked her clergyman whether there was any possibility of his sermons being published, and he answered, "Perhaps posthumously." Replied she: "Oh, how nice! And the sooner the better!"

Asked by his psychiatrist whether he had any pet hostilities, he demurred, "Oh, no. I just love animals."

He's fathering a fifth child after four daughters in a row, because the doctor keeps telling him he needs a little sun and air.

She told the bank teller, "I want to make this withdrawal from my husband's half of our joint account."

He's so dumb he thinks that the English Channel is a British TV station . . . that a naturalist is a crapshooter who throws sevens . . . that the Kentucky Derby is a hat . . . that *sic transit* is being sick on an ocean voyage . . . that syntax is the money the church collects from sinners . . . that the St. Louis Cardinals are appointed by the Pope . . . that a cortege is what you buy for your wife on her anniversary.

Entertainers

His audience couldn't have been colder if he had performed in the morgue.

What an actress! Even if she were cast as Lady Godiva, the horse would steal the show.

His performance is most refreshing. The audience always feels good when they wake up.

He went on right after the monkey act and everyone thought it was an encore.

The audience would have loved her voice except for two things —their ears.

As a musician, he should have kept his dissonance.

Ever since he's been on the air, people are tempted to stop breathing it.

He sang one of his numbers during a thunderstorm. To the audience, it sounded like hail.

He claims he took his piano lessons through a correspondence course. He must have lost a lot of lessons in the mail.

He plays just like Van Cliburn—he uses both hands.

If anyone ever belonged at the top of the ladder in the theatre, it's he—helping the stage hands hang a curtain.

After her performance, they gave her the off-key to the city.

He was egged on to acting by ambition and egged off by the audience.

After that performance, if he had any enemies in the audience, he got even with them.

People wait in line at every one of his performances—to get out.

His most recent tour was a big success—he outran every audience.

He could be more successful if he were given the right vehicle —a truck.

As an M.C., he's an outstanding Massacre of Ceremonies.

As an entertainer, he's half comedian and half wit.

He claims his performance was unprepared and unrehearsed. He might have added that it was also uncalled-for.

His performance was up to his usual substandard.

He gave a soon-to-be-forgotten performance.

He's one of those highstrung actors who should be strung even higher.

If Nero played the fiddle the way this fellow does, no wonder they burned Rome.

He thinks he has a finished act. There's no doubt about it— his act is really finished.

He was flattered when a man in the audience applauded—but the guy was only slapping his head to keep awake.

He used to be an architect, and he's still drawing poor houses.

Some actors can stop a show—he's good at slowing it up.

After his performance, the audience clamored for him to come back, but he didn't dare.

As a comedian, he has a repertoire of six jokes all told—and oh! told and told.

The curtain rose on his performance at 8:30. The audience rose at 8:40.

Last night's performance proved beyond doubt that he's going to go far—the audience chased him five miles.

He's such a ham, he'd feel at home between two slices of bread.

He may be a tenor, but he's overpaid if he gets more than a fiver.

She claims she sings by ear. Unfortunately, that's the way her audience listens.

She's a singer who's destined to go far—and the sooner the better.

Her act goes over like a pregnant woman doing a pole-vault.

The way she carries a tune she seems to be staggering under the load.

Such a voice! She couldn't carry a tune if it had handles.

The trouble with her solo is that it's so high.

She's had a very expensive musical education—her father was sued by five neighbors.

She has a wide range—from a high C to a low V.

She has a large repertoire—and that tight dress she wears sure shows it off.

She gives a soap opera performance that's real corn on the sob.

His audiences always look more like posses or juries.

He gave a down-to-earth performance, and the critics buried it.

He could make a lot of stage, TV, and film stars take back seats—if he drove a cab.

She gives a very moving performance. Long before she's finished, half the audience has already moved out to the lobby.

She sang a very sad number. In fact, the way she sang it, it was pitiful.

His name should always be up on a marquee in bright lights— so that theatregoers can avoid the shows he's in.

Movies and TV programs would be greatly improved if they shot fewer films and more actors like him.

His performance might have gone over better if the seats in the theatre weren't so bad. They faced the stage.

Egotists

If he should ever change his faith, it'll be because he no longer thinks he's God.

If he could ever get anyone to love him as much as he loves himself, it would be history's greatest romance.

She thinks she's a siren, but she looks more like a false alarm.

He always wants to be the center of attraction. Whenever he goes to a funeral, he's sorry he isn't the corpse.

He has an alarm clock and a phone that don't ring—they applaud.

He'll never get married. He can't find a woman who will love him as much as he does.

Someone should tell him the difference between pulling his weight and throwing it around.

He doesn't read books, look at TV, or listen to the radio—they take his mind off himself.

The hardest secret she's ever had to keep is her opinion of herself.

Her body has gone to her head.

He's too puffed up to remember that Napoleon is now a cake and Bismarck is a herring.

Success is going to his head, but it's bound to be a short visit.

He brags that he's sitting on top of the world. Someone should remind him that it turns every twenty-four hours.

He stands high in his own mind, but he's still a long way from the top.

Success turned his head, and it left him facing in the wrong direction.

He's one of those big-shot executives who has to have two desks—one for each foot.

All he needs to boost his ego is a swivel chair.

He likes well-informed employees—those whose views coincide with his own.

He knows when an idea is good—when it's one of his.

One of these days he'll fracture his pride in a fall over his own bluff.

He's the type who talks big and performs small.

Her head is like a weather vane on top of a house. It's easily turned by the slightest wind.

The only time she won't look in a mirror is when she's pulling out of a parking space.

Money has brought him everything except sense and humility.

He thinks he's worth a lot of money just because he has it.

He's never been known to say an unkind thing about anyone —that's because he only talks about himself.

Just get into a conversation with him, and the night will have a thousand I's.

Success hasn't changed him one bit. He's the same stinker he always was.

He's looking for a woman who will look up to him as smart and handsome. What he needs is a nearsighted midget.

He'll never install machines that can do employees' jobs. When he talks, they couldn't listen and nod.

He can pat himself on the back better than a contortionist.

When he brags that he's a self-made man you can't help wondering who interrupted him.

He claims that he's self-made. Too bad he left out the working parts.

If he's *really* self-made, he has no one to blame but himself.

He boasts that he's a self-educated man. There's no question at all about his being his own toot-er.

If he tells you he's a self-made man, just accept his apology and let it go at that.

He keeps reminding everyone that he came upstairs in the world as a self-made man. He must have been born in a cellar.

When it comes to seeing his own faults, he's blinder than an earthworm in a London fog.

He's an eel who thinks he's a whale.

He's going through life with his horn stuck.

Success has not only gone to his head, but to his mouth as well.

His big bankroll is only matched by his big head and his big stomach.

Because this is the machine age, he thinks he has to be the big wheel.

He's a bachelor. He thinks the only justified marriage on record was the one that produced him.

He could take a great weight off his mind—by discarding that halo.

No wonder he suffers from migraine—his halo is on too tight.

He's so egotistical he even signs his name to anonymous letters.

One thing he'll never be in danger of—delusions of humility.

It's a good thing he doesn't have to pay taxes on what *he* thinks he's worth.

He has a mirror on the bathroom ceiling so he can watch himself gargle.

He can get up in the air faster than a rocket with his inflated ego.

His conceit is in inverse ration to his lack of ability.

He's always singing his own praise, but it's an unaccompanied solo.

His bragging is simply the loud patter of little feats.

He gets carried away with his own importance. The trouble is, not far enough.

He always hires people who like what he likes—him.

If you've never heard a good word about him, it's only because you haven't heard him talking about himself.

He's such a big gun in the office they're planning to fire him.

He's master of the art of making deep noises from the chest sound like important messages from the brain.

His greatest admirer is his wife's husband.

He's sure if he hadn't been born, the world would wonder why.

If you're not talking about *him*, he's not listening.

He overrates his value to his firm. Even a pair of shoe trees can fill his shoes.

He always envies his new acquaintances—imagine meeting someone great like him!

He needs two private offices—one for his head.

He's the type who swells in prosperity and shrinks in adversity.

He's a big problem to his psychiatrist—he's too big for the couch.

He denies he's conceited. He just happens to have a high opinion of people with ability, good looks, and personality.

He thinks he's cooking with gas. The trouble is, he inhales some of it.

He's never taken a hot shower. It clouds the mirror.

Failures

He has just made the list of the nation's Ten Best Nobodies.

He never made Who's Who, but he's sure to be in "Who's Through."

During the short time he's been on the job, he has displaced genuine ability.

He works his gums talking himself into a job, and gums the works afterward.

Maybe he had the right aim in life, but he's sure run out of ammunition.

He's money-mad. He's never had any money—and that makes him mad.

He's so seedy, he trembles every time he passes a canary.

His boss would gladly pay him what he's worth—but it's against the Minimum Wage Law.

He was voted by his graduation class as the man most likely to go to seed.

Not even the Missing Persons Bureau could help him find himself. He has that certain nothing.

He always takes his salary to the bank. It's too little to go by itself.

He's selling furniture for a living—his own.

He's been up against the wall so much, the handwriting is on him.

His aptitude test shows that his only aptitude is for taking aptitude tests.

He's always sounding off about capital and labor, but he's never had any capital and never did any labor.

His boss keeps telling him, "Your salary raise will become effective just as soon as you do.

He hatches a lot of ideas—the trouble is, he doesn't hitch them.

He sat around so long dreaming of when his ship would come in, his salary got docked.

His boss was disturbed when he told him he was quitting next week—he'd hoped it was this week.

He stayed awake nights figuring how to succeed. It would have been better if he had stayed awake days.

He left his last job because he was told to do something he didn't like—look for another job.

He has always itched for success, but he's never been willing to scratch for it.

There's lots less to him than meets the eye.

He can't tell the difference between working up steam and generating a fog.

He has always watched the clock, so he's still only one of the hands.

He's always been one jump ahead of the other fellow—the trouble is, he's never been headed in the right direction.

He's going steady now with a girl who's different from other girls—she's the only girl who'll go with him.

He's one guy who has ulcers without being a success.

The only thing that keeping his ear to the ground has ever done for him is to limit his vision.

He's *really* in debt! He has more attachments on him than a vacuum cleaner.

He often tells his boss how to run his business. Then his boss leaves in his chauffeured Cadillac, and he takes the subway home.

He's always suggesting campaigns for the future. A few more ideas like those and he won't have any future.

His motto is "All things come to him who waits." The trouble is, he doesn't know what he's waiting for.

A pickpocket once tried to snatch some money from his pocket, but all he got was practice.

He has five keen senses—sight, smell, taste, touch, and hearing. All he lacks is *horse* and *common*.

He worked his head off, and finally got to the top of the ladder —only to find that he'd leaned it against the wrong wall.

He knows that it's not whether you win or lose but how you play the game that counts. Now all he has to find out is: How do you get into the game?

Nobody can call him a quitter—he's always been fired from every job he's had.

He has so many irons in the fire, no wonder the fire is out.

He's making as much headway as a snake making love to a buggy whip.

He's like a fence—just runs around a lot without getting anywhere.

The easiest thing he ever ran into was debt.

Half-doing has been his undoing.

He had an itch to succeed—and got loused up just thinking about it.

His efforts count for as much as the speed of a runaway horse.

He can at least be thankful that his job is too crummy for any self-respecting electronic machine to take it away from him.

If his life's story is ever written, it will be about the Man Who Started at the Bottom—and *stayed* there.

Whenever opportunity knocks, instead of getting off his feet to open the door, he complains about the noise.

Watching an opulent-looking man stepping into his chauffeured Cadillac, he sighed, "There but for me go I."

He has a positive genius for taking a bankroll and running it into a shoestring.

Sending him out to do a man's job is like sending a tadpole to tackle a whale.

He had the world by the tail—too bad he couldn't swing it.

Anytime you find him with his ear to the ground it's just because he's looking for a contact lens.

He's always dropping the ball and then complaining about the way the ball bounces.

He's been waiting for something to turn up. He should have started long ago with his own shirtsleeves.

At least you have to hand it to him for imagination. He thinks he can run the business better than the boss.

He's waited so long for his ship to come in, his pier has collapsed.

His last satisfactory letter of reference read: "—— worked for us for one month. He is no longer working for us. We are satisfied."

He took an aptitude test to find what he was best suited for. It showed the thing he was best suited for was *retirement*.

At 20 he knew nothing; at 40 he's done nothing; at 60 he'll have nothing.

Here's one guy who never has ups and downs—he always goes around in circles.

He was cut out to be a genius. Too bad someone didn't take the trouble to put the pieces together.

As an infant, his mother paid nursemaids ready cash to push him around in his buggy—and he's been pushed for ready cash ever since.

He'll never be a financial success. He's always coming up with ideas for items that are high-priced, non-habit-forming or non-tax-deductible.

He wanted to be a lawyer badly, and he realized his ambition— he became a bad lawyer.

Fallen angels

She came to the big city as just a slip of a girl, and she's been slipping ever since.

She had a sylphlike figure. Too bad she didn't keep it to her sylph.

She agreed to be a guy's intended. Too bad she didn't know what he intended.

A fellow made improper advances to her in a plane, and she didn't say "Stop or I'll chute!"

She went out with a sailor, not knowing he was a wolf in ship's clothing. Then she dated a G.I.—and didn't call a halt.

She has very little will power, and even less won't power.

A chap told her he was bringing her home to Maw, but he brought her home to paw.

Her boy friend said, "Let's get married or something." Too bad she didn't say, "Let's get married or nothing."

She could speak five languages, but couldn't say "no" in any one of them.

A fellow once fought for her honor. Too bad she didn't.

The boys tell her she's the salt of the earth, and they pepper her with propositions.

She was a well-bred girl—all the fellows buttered her up.

She was just the village belle who wasn't tolled, so she went from good to bed.

She closed her eyes one night when a fellow kissed her—she should have closed his.

Someone should have told her that lots of things have been started by kisses—especially *little things*.

She summers in the Adirondacks, winters in Palm Beach, and falls everywhere.

That fur coat does a lot for her—but then, she did a lot for it.

She skated on thin ice, and ended up in hot water.

They told her that if there was a cherry in it, it wasn't intoxicating.

She went out with chaps who were strict gentlemen from the word stop. Too bad she never learned the word.

She was just a little lamb who didn't give a fellow the cold shoulder, so she came home at 4:00 A.M. with a sheepish grin.

She could hardly wait until she got married—in fact, she didn't.

When a man bought her champagne and got her high as a kite, she didn't suspect there was a string attached to it.

A guy's overtures to her in his convertible drove her to distraction—too bad she didn't walk back.

A fellow said, "I look into your eyes, and I want to teach them the language of love." He found them very willing pupils.

She struggled for years to get a mink coat. Then she stopped struggling—and got it.

A chap gave her candy, and it meant he was thinking about her. He gave her flowers, and it meant he was smitten by her. Then he gave her some fine lingerie, and it meant business.

She was a good girl until she stopped whispering those sweet nothing-doings in fellows' ears.

She went out on a date with a boy friend who took a camera along—she sure was a snap.

She permits fellows liberties only within certain limits—city and state.

The only thing she ever gives is in.

She went on a picnic with a boyfriend, but didn't go with certain provisions.

She was as green as grass, and it didn't take the fellows long to weed out her objections.

She went out with a guy who was a magician, and he turned into a shady lane.

All the boys have to do is put two and two together, and they have her number.

She runs the gamut of emotions—from yes to yes.

When the average girl says "no," she means it—but she's not average.

She claims if her parents had told her about the birds and the bees she wouldn't have got stung.

She went out with a fellow who said he could read her like a book. She didn't realize he liked to read in bed.

A fellow asked her to be his mistress, and she reclined to do so.

She was just a local girl who everybody made good.

She was an inexperienced secretary who didn't know how to keep her boss from ending a sentence with a proposition.

There's nothing complex about her—anyone can grasp her.

She started her sex education with a book titled *What Every Girl Should Know*. It wasn't too long before she was reading *The Care and Feeding of Infants*.

Whenever she was being seduced, she tried hard to remember her mother's warning about men, but she couldn't seem to recoil at the moment.

Features

He's the kind of fellow that girls dream of every night—it's better than seeing him in the light.

She looks good after a fashion—after a couple of Old-Fashioneds.

Looks aren't everything; in her case, they aren't anything.

When she goes down to the waterfront, even the tugboats stop whistling.

He has a very sympathetic face. It has everyone's sympathy.

There's only one trouble with his face—it shows.

She's on the 144th day of a 14-day beauty plan.

When she comes out of a beauty parlor, she looks as though she believes it.

What a face! He has to sneak up on the mirror to shave.

She had a coming-out party, but they made her go back again.

He looks much better without your glasses.

He's always concerned about losing face. He shouldn't be—it would be a decided improvement.

When he was born, folks came from miles around to look at him—they didn't know what he was.

He looks even worse than his passport photograph.

He was missing once, but his wife didn't go to the Missing Persons Bureau—they wouldn't believe it!

He looks like Grant. General—not Cary.

He was a war baby. His folks took just one look at him, and they started fighting.

He's smarter than he looks. That at least is reassuring.

He should only go out on Halloween—it's the only time he can pass as normal.

He should join the Ku Klux Klan—he would look a lot better with a hood over his head.

A photographer took his picture, but never developed it. He was afraid to be alone with it in the darkroom.

He looks like a canceled five-cent stamp.

His features don't seem to know the importance of teamwork.

A man's best weapons for attracting women are his physical charms. He should be arrested for carrying concealed weapons.

She appeared recently in a beauty contest, and got several offers—from plastic surgeons.

She smears so much cold cream and oil all over her body that she slides out of bed.

She's tried to get a man—but without avail. Maybe she'd better wear one.

At a holiday party, they hung her and kissed the mistletoe.

She has to wait until winter to get a chap on her hands.

A fellow told a friend of his that he'd dig up a girl for him, and evidently he did—he brought her.

A fellow took her out once and announced to his friends: "Was that a girl! Was that a girl! That's what everyone kept asking—Was that a girl?"

When she goes into a cornfield, she scares the crows so badly that they bring back the corn they took the year before.

A Martian took one look at her with her thick cold cream, curlers, and hairnet, and exclaimed, "Lantzman!"

She's not exactly bad-looking. There's just a little blemish between her ears—her face.

If a woman's face is her fortune, she'll never have to pay income tax.

Some generous person should give her a kitten—she could use a new puss.

She' had scores of fellows at her feet. They look up at her face, and they're promptly at her feet again.

She's an identical twin, but fellows can tell them apart—her brother has a mole on his cheek.

She looks like a million—every year of it.

Maybe her makeup is an improvement over Mother Nature, but it sure isn't fooling Father Time.

She can easily protect herself from Peeping Toms—all she has to do is leave the shades up.

Everyone says she's an angel fallen from the skies. Too bad she happened to land on her face.

After half a day in a beauty parlor, she still hasn't been worked on—they're still busy giving her an estimate.

As a blind date, fellows look forward to meeting a vision. She's a vision all right—a sight.

She has a bleaches-and-cream complexion.

Her complexion can best be described as seasick green.

She's had her face lifted so many times, she talks through her nose.

She's as wrinkled as a last year's apple.

She's trying a cream that's advertised as able to remove wrinkles from a prune. It hasn't helped her face much, but she sure has some smooth prunes.

She had to have her face lifted—it was a case of drastic surgery.

Her face was lifted the other day, but the crook who took it is bringing it back.

She's had plastic surgery on her face, but it doesn't look any different than it did $1000 ago.

She's never had her face lifted. She was having it done once, but the derrick broke.

Time may be a great healer, but she'd do better with a plastic surgeon.

Every once in awhile she gets a mud pack. It improves her looks for a few days—then the mud falls off.

With all that makeup on, she doesn't look like an old woman anymore—she looks like an old man.

That can't be the face he was born with—it must be a retread.

He has a face like a flower—a cauliflower.

With a face like his, he should sue his parents for damages.

He must be using gunpowder on his face—it sure looks shot.

He has so many chins, he should be careful not to burp—it would start a ripple.

He has so many chins, you can't be sure which one he's going to talk out of next.

Even her double chin has a double chin. Her husband would tickle her under the chin—if he could decide which one.

People look at her and exclaim: "Ah, those eyes, those lips, those chin!"

She has two mink wraps—one for each chin.

You can't blame her for getting mad at people when they tell her to keep her best chin forward.

She needs bookmarks to find her chin.

Her mouth is so small, she has to use a shoehorn to take an aspirin.

He has such a big mouth, he can sing a duet all by himself.

His mouth is so big, when he yawns his ears disappear.

He has a nice head on his shoulders. But it would look better on a neck.

He's been offered a good price for his head, for the top of a totem pole.

Some of his features he got from his mother, and his ears from his father, but that nose could only have been his own idea.

He has a Roman nose—it roams all over his face.

He has a fine set of tooth.

His teeth are like the Ten Commandments—all broken.

He has Pullman teeth—one upper and one lower.

He goes to a dentist twice a year—once for each tooth.

He's a very resolute person—he keeps a stiff upper plate.

He bit into an apple and broke three teeth, but he isn't too concerned. He still has three left.

He has a heart of gold, and teeth to match.

His teeth are his own. He just made the last payment on them.

As a blonde, she's a brunette with a top secret.

Any resemblance between her and a blonde is purely peroxidental.

She uses fine rouges to bring out her cheekbones; good mascara to bring out her eyes; good lipsticks to bring out her lips—but when she gives a good sneeze, it brings out her teeth.

Her hair has been dyed so often, her dandruff is technicolored.

She's a suicide blonde—dyed by her own hand.

She has so many wrinkles on her forehead, she has to screw her hat on.

She's not exactly fading—she's dyeing.

If you put a stick on her hairdo, you could mop the floor with it.

He's so bald, you have to wear sunglasses to look at him in a bright light.

He has waving hair—it's waving goodbye.

He's not baldheaded—he just has flesh-colored hair.

His hair is departed in the middle.

He has a crew haircut. The only trouble is, the crew is bailing out.

From a short distance away, it looks like his neck is blowing bubblegum.

There's one proverb that really depresses him: "Hair today, gone tomorrow."

He was very ambitious, but the only thing about him that has come out on top is his hair.

Barbers don't charge him for cutting his hair—they charge him for searching for it.

He can swat flies with his ears.

From the front he looks like a loving cup.

Ears? When he stands in a restaurant waiting for a table, in no time five hats are hung on them.

The only time you can see a head like his is in a bag of oats.

He's so nearsighted, when he can't fall asleep he counts elephants.

He kisses the cat and puts his wife out.

He walks into a closet and says, "Down!"

In the office he never stops working for even a minute—he can't see when the boss is approaching.

He once picked up a snake to kill a stick.

He has to have contact lenses to find his spectacles.

He belongs to an organization of nearsighted men. They have

a theme song: "I've Lost My Glasses—I Wonder Who's Kissing Her Now."

His eyes are so askew, he can watch a tennis match without moving his head.

Her right eye must be real fascinating—her left eye keeps looking at it all the time.

There may not be much character on his face, but what a face on that character!

A face like a bottle of warts . . . like a busted sofa . . . like a smoked herring . . . like a squeezed orange.

She says her face is her fortune. That woman is full of hard-luck stories.

Figures

HERS

She has a real faminine look.

All her sweater does for her is make her itch.

That sweater doesn't do her too much good. The way she looks in it, the wool looked better on the sheep.

She'll never be a bonnie lassie as long as she has that bony chassis.

She just doesn't have the backbone to join a nudist colony—not with that knobby spine.

When she drinks tomato juice, she looks like a thermometer.

A fellow with a skinny girl friend like her doesn't get around very much.

She resorts to all sorts of devices to fill out her figure—and it's a sham dame.

She's straight and marrow.

She admits she has a boyish figure—and that's straight from the shoulder.

There's enough cotton in her sweater to start a goodsized first-aid station.

If it wasn't for her Adam's apple, she wouldn't have any shape at all.

There's only one trouble with her figure. It comes out where it should go in, and where it comes out it stays right where it is.

She doesn't have to take a back seat to anyone—and she has the back seat to prove it.

Her girdle is the outstanding example of the difference between fact and figure.

She looks like a piano. If she weren't so upright, she'd be grand.

Now that her husband has enough money to buy her dresses for a fancy figure, she no longer has one.

Her little daughter was once asked, "What will you do, dear, when you're as big as your mother?" and she answered, "Diet."

She's a light eater. As soon as it gets light, she starts eating.

She's been on several diets. The only thing that got thin was her temper.

She eats like a bird—a peck at a time.

Those between-meal snacks are the pauses that reflesh her.

She's been on a coconut and banana diet. It hasn't reduced her, but you should see her climb trees.

She went through with that 14-day diet, but all she lost was two weeks.

Her problem isn't just taking off weight, but rearranging it.

She's much too big in the first place, and in the second place, too.

She's a well-reared female.

She's a real big-hearted woman—with hips to match.

What a nice figure she had!—fifty pounds ago.

With a figure like hers, she has a brilliant career ahead—as a model for slipcovers.

They say figures don't lie, but her girdles sure condense the truth.

She claims to be one of the "400," but she doesn't look a pound over 350.

She's a real Oomph gal—when she sits on a sofa, it goes oomph.

She'll never take your breath away unless she takes a lot of that breadth away.

She's really watching her weight—watching it go up.

Everytime she steps on a scale, she's reminded of one of President Roosevelt's famous phrase: *A gain—and a gain—and a gain.*

You really enjoy seeing her laughing—so much of her has a good time.

She doesn't realize that while some women may look attractive in slacks, that doesn't hold true for the bulk of them.

Once she did have an hourglass figure, but the sands of time ran down—to the bottom.

Her girdles and corsets give her an hourglass figure, but without them—Big Ben.

For the past two weeks, she's been doing a lot of horseback riding, and she's taken off ten pounds—from the horse.

She's very prominent in the best of society circles, and around the hips.

Whenever she sings, you wonder how a little aria can come out of such a big area.

Examining her, an absentminded doctor said, "Open your mouth and say moo."

She once had a million-dollar figure. Too bad inflation set in.

She's looking for a girdle to support her in the manner to which she's accustomed.

When she walked down the aisle with her groom, they had to walk single file.

She's putting on so much weight, she's running out of places to hide it.

Trying hard to get on a bus, she snapped to the man in back of her, "If you were half a man, you'd help me onto this." He answered, "If you were half a lady, you wouldn't need any help."

HIS

He has a military figure—some of it goes to the front.

He's a do-it-yourself man. He made a bay window with a knife and fork.

It's not the minutes he takes at the table that put all that weight on him—it's the seconds.

He's real unhappy because he has only one mouth.

His indigestion is due to his inability to adjust a square meal to a round stomach.

Prosperity has not only gone to his head, but to his stomach.

He has a stomach without a memory.

He has T.B.—Twin Bellies.

You can always depend on him. With his avoirdupois he'll never stoop to anything low.

He's a man who carries a lot of weight—in his stomach.

He can take a shower without getting his feet wet.

The President of the United States should appoint him chairman of the government's Physical Fatness program.

If he's not overweight, then he's certainly six inches too short.

He's scared of his own shadow—it's beginning to look like a mob.

He's one guy who doesn't need a build-up—he has enough as it is

When he has his shoes shined, he has to take the bootblack's word for it.

There's one thing bigger than his stomach—his appetite.

He's stopped dancing. He can't find a concave woman for a partner.

He certainly cuts a wide swath among women.

He quit his job as a food taster—didn't get enough time off for lunch.

His posterior isn't just a seat—it's a whole county seat.

He got on a talk-your-weight scale, and the voice called out: "One at a time, please!"

Does he love to eat! His stomach always comes first—especially when going through a door.

He got on one of those scales that stamps the weight on a card. When the card came out, it read: "Please return later—*alone!*"

He can sit around a table all by himself.

He snapped to his wife: "Where is all the grocery money going?" And she said, "If you really want to know, stand sidewise and look in the mirror."

There are just two things he can't eat for dinner—breakfast and lunch.

He's not only a heavy but a fast eater. He's starting on his desert before the echo of his soup has died away.

He has an optimistic stomach and a pessimistic digestion.

He's on a garlic diet. He hasn't lost any weight, but quite a few friends.

Lots of people in town knew him when he had only one stomach and one chin.

He always has intimate little dinners for two. Trouble is, no one else eats them with him.

Lately he's tried tranquilizers to reduce. He hasn't lost any weight, but he *has* stopped worrying about being beefy and paunchy.

He must have grown up when meat was cheap.

He's tried many diets, but let's face it—he's a poor loser.

He has a big heart, and a stomach to match.

He's a man with an outstanding personality, and it's all in his bay window.

THE SHAPE HE'S IN

He looks like his dear departed brother—ten years after he departed.

Better bodies than his can be found in a used car lot.

You take one look at him, and wonder whether there were any other survivors.

He looks like he'd been sent for and couldn't come.

He loves nature, despite what nature did to him.

The only reason he doesn't beat his breast in time of trouble is that he can't find it.

He's one guy who'll never be a blood donor—in fact, he's not even a blood owner.

He must have gone to the blood bank and forgotten to say "when."

Following his physical, he asked the doctor, "How do I stand?" Replied the doctor, "I don't know—it's a miracle."

He's taken vitamins A, B, C, D, E, F, and G, and still looks like H.

As an insomniac, he takes yellow, green, blue, and red sleeping tablets before retiring. He still doesn't get much sleep, but at least when he does he dreams in Technicolor.

He looks like he gave his pallbearers the slip.

When he sneezes, it's really germ warfare.

On his wedding day, they didn't throw rice as he left the church—they threw vitamins.

His insurance man takes a look at him and turns pale.

He's the perfect picture of health. Unfortunately, the frame isn't.

Maybe he isn't quite ready yet to kick off, but his doctor doesn't think it'll do him any good to start a magazine serial.

He's seeking a new type of insurance company—the Black and Blue Cross.

A doctor told him he's "as sound as a dollar"—and he hasn't figured out yet that he's half dead.

One time a cop accosted his wife as she was out in the street with him, and inquired, "Lady, did you report this accident?"

His doctor has just advised him: "In your condition, you'll have to give up wine and women, but you can sing as much as you want to."

He's got a ringing in his ears like a bellhop.

As the doctor compared his latest X rays with last year's X rays, he asked, "No worse?" The doc took a good look and answered, "No man."

With that bad liver because he's a good liver he's likely to be a short liver.

Not for him are night clubs—he patronizes a spot called the Slipped Discotheque.

He claims he's taking a strength- and health-building correspondence school course. They must have forgotten to mail him the muscles.

He's so thin, it takes two of him to make a shadow.

They had to make room for him on a transcontinental flight—so they removed ten airmail letters.

When he takes his clothes off, it's like watching the unveiling of a golf stick.

He's been offered a job modeling for thermometers.

When he wears a black suit, he resembles a closed umbrella.

His wife says exactly the same about him as she does about astronauts and male movie stars. She looks at one of them and says, "This is a man!" And she looks at him and says, "This is a man?"

Flat tires

Her boy friends like her just the way she is—single.

A square like him they could build a town around.

She's one girl you like to bring home to Mother—her mother.

She can trace her ancestors back to the wallflower.

For years now, she's been planning a runaway marriage with her boyfriend—but every time they plan, he runs away.

She's a real "It" girl. People take one look at her and ask, "What is it?"

He goes out with very religious girls. They take a look at him and exclaim, "Oh, God!"

She swears she's never been kissed. She can hardly be blamed for swearing.

She prays every night, "Dear Lord, I don't ask a thing for myself. Just send my parents a son-in-law."

Her last boyfriend is wondering who's kissing her—and why.

Even at a charity ball, fellows don't ask her to dance.

She thinks she knows now when she's getting married. A fellow told her it will be a cold day in December when he marries her.

The boys don't call her attractive, nor do they call her homely —they just don't call her.

She's had a love seat for three years, and one half of it is still new.

She's willing to enter into the give-and-take of marriage. The trouble is, she can't find anyone who'll take what she has to give.

With those low-cut dresses it's obvious she's out to catch a man—but all she catches is a cold.

She has to change her seat four or five times in a movie theatre before she can get someone to annoy her.

She's never been able to train a guy's voice to have an engagement ring in it.

Every night when she climbs into bed, she sighs, "Ah-men!"

She was two-thirds married once. She was there, the minister was there, but the groom didn't show up.

She's in the prim of life.

She's such a prude, she blindfolds herself while taking a bath.

She won't even stay in the same room with a clock that's fast.

She won't even look at anything with a naked eye.

In school she refused to do improper fractions.

She even blindfolds the goldfish when she takes a bath.

Fellows only take her to the movies when they want to see the picture—and they sit in the orchestra.

A guy took her out recently—an outstanding member of the Humane Society.

She's just met a fellow who's unquestionably her type—he's alive and breathing.

She not only kisses a fellow to hold him, she has to hold him to kiss him.

She's not like some girls who rush into marriage—she's waiting for someone to ask her.

One time she was engaged and she and her boyfriend were half serious about getting married. She was and he wasn't.

Lately she's been hanging around draft boards waiting for rejects.

She's having a disagreement with her fiancé. She wants a big church wedding—and he doesn't want to get married.

She likes to be looked at and up to, and fails on both counts.

He's the answer to a maiden's prayer. No wonder so few girls are praying nowadays.

He has a leaning toward blondes—but they keep pushing him back.

When he sits on a couch with a girl and the lights go out, he spends the rest of the evening repairing the fuse.

If his girl friend puts out the light when they're sitting on the couch, he gets up and goes home—says he can take a hint.

With a bit more effort on his part, he could be a nonenity.

He's the type that has that certain nothing.

Any woman who goes out with him sure must love the simpler things in life.

He's gotten all his letters back from his latest girl friend, marked "4th Class Male."

He has as much passion as an exercise in calculus, and as much romance as a stockyard.

His father wanted a boy, his mother wanted a girl—and they're both satisfied.

He asked a girl for "just three little words that will make me walk on air." She obliged him—with "Go hang yourself."

So far as women are concerned, he's nonhabit-forming.

He claims that women are shorter than they used to be. No wonder—they shrink from his touch.

He says he can marry any girl he pleases. The trouble is, he doesn't please anybody.

He's the type who attracts raving beauties—escapees from the booby hatch.

For years he's been looking for a girl who's tall and willowy. Now he'll settle for one who's short and willing.

Goat-getters

He thinks he is the very apex of creation. Actually, he's the ex-ape.

Whoever first said "Love thy neighbor" never had one like him.

If Moses had known him, there would positively have been another commandment.

He's the type you'd like to run into sometime—when you're driving and he's walking.

Some people are born great, some become great—he just grates.

He has a dual personality—Dr. Heckle and Mr. Snide.

He's the kind who can really creep into your heart and creep into your mind. In fact, you'll never meet a bigger creep.

He's a square shooter—one of those squares you'd love to shoot.

Whoever made that pest should have kept the mold and thrown *him* away.

There's nothing wrong with him that a miracle couldn't cure.

Two women once fought a duel over him to decide who'd get him. One got him in the leg and the other in the arm.

One of these days he's sure to be arrested for impersonating a human being.

If he ever needs a friend, he'll have to get a dog.

The only way he'll ever avoid having enemies is to outlive them.

He's one person who'd make a perfect stranger.

He recently asked someone for a dime to call a friend. "Here's twenty cents," he was told. "Call *all* your friends!"

He'll never get sick—no germ could stand him.

There are no two people alike, and everyone who knows him is glad of it.

He hasn't been himself lately—everyone has noticed the improvement.

He's such a pain in everyone's neck, the aspirin people are considering giving him a royalty.

When he was born, they fired twenty-one guns. Too bad they missed.

He comes from a really brave family. They just didn't know the meaning of "quit" until he was born.

When the stork brought him, he flew around the zoo for a week before he had the nerve to drop him off at his parents' house.

His folks took one look at him when he was born, and hired a lawyer immediately to find a loophole in the birth certificate.

His father passed out from sheer fatigue—from throwing rocks at the stork. He should have kept the cigars and given *him* away.

People have watched him—man and boy—for many years, and they don't like him any better as a man than they did as a boy.

Everyone confuses him with a hockey player. They tell him, "You stink on ice."

The next time you'll meet anyone like him it will be during a siege of heebie-jeebies or delirium tremens.

The only time in his life that he was ever popular was as a kid in school. He gave all the kids measles just before exams.

He's in no danger of being kidnaped—he hasn't a friend who could be contacted for ransom arrangements.

He has only two faults—everything he says and everything he does.

When he calls you on the phone and says, "Guess who this is," you don't have to guess what he is.

He makes you wish his parents had never met.

People like him don't just grow on trees—they swing from them.

No one really knows what makes him so obnoxious, but whatever it is, it works.

He's nasty, repulsive, repugnant, disagreeable, offensive, belligerent, pugnacious, and antagonistic—and those are his good points.

He thinks he's out of this world—and everyone wishes he were.

He's one of Nature's disagreeable blunders.

He'll waste his time doing his Christmas shopping early. The odds are definitely against his having any friends left by Christmas.

There's no middle ground where he's concerned—you either hate or detest him.

A number of his acquaintances have named their first ulcers after him.

He has grown up to be the kind of a fellow his mother warned him not to associate with.

He's a man of many parts—and it's a lousy assembly job.

Bees are much too busy for birth control, which makes it understandable why there are so many sons of bees like him around.

His girl friend demanded a refund on the perfume she had purchased because all it attracted was *him*.

You really have to know him to depreciate him.

He's a real smellebrity.

He's in the public eye all right—as a cinder.

He's made quite a name for himself, but his acquaintances are too gentlemanly to tell him what that name is.

He is one person who should speak well of his enemies—after all, *he made them.*

He's the kind of guy you'd rebuff even if you were bleeding to death and he had the only available tourniquet.

Scientists who have studied him go even further than Darwin did. They say people like him have already started on the return trip.

A newspaper erroneously printed a notice that he had died. Next day they announced: "We regret that the notice of his death was not true."

He's fond of travel. He's always going from city to city, greeting old enemies and making new.

If a revolution ever breaks out in this country, it will be everybody against *him.*

The chief trouble with human nature is that there are too many guys like him connected with it.

He's the outstanding justification for mercy killings.

He thinks everyone worships the ground he crawled out of.

"You remind me of the ocean," a girl told him. "Oh," he asked, "you mean wild, restless and romantic?" "No," she said, "you just make me sick."

With his money, he has just about everything a girl could want. The only trouble is, he goes with it.

He's the kind of guy who can give a headache to an aspirin.

When he dies, they'll bury him face down—so he'll see where he's going.

On his demise, a great many people will attend his funeral—to make absolutely sure he's dead.

His death notice is sure not to appear in the obituary columns, but under "Public Improvements."

Whoever eulogizes him will undoubtedly say, "He was a fine man, a good citizen, a great friend—*provided he's really dead.*"

In psychoanalysis he finally found his real self—only to discover that he stood for everything he disliked.

He's the type you like better the more you see him less.

If he ever has his life to live over again, he shouldn't do it.

Gold diggers

She has a split personality. Whenever she meets a man with money, she's ready to split it with him.

She doesn't care especially for a man's company—unless he owns it.

She's a real athlete—always ready to play ball with a man with a bankroll.

She enjoyed swimming with a playboy banker. Now she can float a loan.

If you think postage rates are high now, you should see what she charges just to play Post Office.

When she strokes men's foreheads, little do they suspect it's their scalps she's after.

She's ready to put her trust in a man—if he'll put his money in trust for her.

Her specialty is promoting well-heeled playboys—thar's gold in them thar heels.

Green is the color that's most restful for her eyes—especially the long green.

She's a girl with a past, and the only way to figure in her future is with a present.

Her idea of a romantic setting is one that has a diamond in it.

She likes men who, when they look at her, make dollar signs run up and down her spine.

Her latest sugar daddy irks her—but after all, it's nice irk, if she can get it.

She doesn't mind if a man loves her and leaves her—if he leaves her enough.

It's not hard to meet her—just open your wallet, and there she is.

Any guy who's foolish enough to write her a love letter, might as well start it, "Darling, and Gentlemen of the Jury."

She likes men who go for stocks and bonds and put their stock in blondes.

She's going around with an eccentric rich guy who's really cracked; but she doesn't mind, so long as he isn't broke.

She drops in occasionally on her sugar daddy to take his wallet for a walk.

When she goes out with a man, she really thinks of his value —his cash surrender value.

No sooner does a fellow lose his capital than she loses her interest.

She has a peculiar idea of fair exchange. A boyfriend gave her an Oldsmobile and she gave him the Dodge.

She likes a four-letter man—whose four letters are enough to convince a jury.

She sure knows what to give a man who has everything—encouragement.

When a fellow goes out with her, his heart may be in the clouds, but her hand is in his pocket.

She knows how to get minks and sables. The same way minks get minks and sables get sables.

She got tired of trying to get a pearl out of an oyster, so she smarted up—and got a diamond out of an old crab.

She specializes in finding dopes who can be easily cleaned by soft soap.

She calls her latest boyfriend Louis, because he's the 14th whose bankroll she has taken.

Her head on a guy's shoulder accomplishes more than his does.

If you should exclaim, "Goodness, what a lovely fur coat," she'll admit that goodness had nothing to do with it.

She has the combination to open her paramour's safe—36-24-36.

She's not interested in every Tom, Dick, and Harry. She's out to get Jack.

With her, romance starts with sentiment and ends with a settlement.

The fellows all call her "the Baseball Girl"—she won't play without a diamond.

She doesn't talk all the time. Sometimes she listens—when money talks.

If you think women aren't explosive, just try dropping one.

Her current inamorato calls her "Resolution"—she's getting harder to keep.

She has no use for men who try to mess up the country's prosperity by living within their income.

When her latest lover broke off their engagement, she didn't take it to heart—she took it to court.

She resembles an insurance policy—both have cash surrender value.

She knows how to make a rich guy stop, look, and loosen.

She doesn't mind if a man doesn't have his name in the Social Register, so long as he has enough in the cash register.

In slang terms, her boyfriends may know their onions when it comes to tomatoes, but she knows her carats.

When friends ask her, "Where have you been keeping yourself?" she answers truthfully, "I haven't."

It doesn't take her long to snare a rich guy—just a little wile.

She was interested in do-re-me and went so-fa.

She's not the least bit interested in go-getters—she looks for already-gotters.

She enjoys being read to—from a bankbook.

When she tells a guy, "I'll never forget the loving things you wrote me," he'd better start looking for a good lawyer.

She's still a child at heart. She likes her sugar daddy to give her blocks to play with—48th to 52nd street.

She wears perfume that brings out the mink in a man without stirring up the wolf.

Her friends wonder who's the rich old geezer they've been seeing her outwit.

She scoffs at the idea of going to a psychiatrist. Why should she lie down on a man's couch, and then pay him?

When she told a man, "I can't learn to love you," he said, "But I have $100,000." Quickly she said, "Give me one more lesson."

She never got anywhere by putting her shoulder to the wheel, so now she puts her head on the shoulder of the man at the Cadillac wheel.

She has a real gift for love-making—usually it's a diamond.

She goes out with sentimental men—the very sight of her brings a lump to their wallets.

Since her latest boyfriend met her, he can't eat, he can't sleep, he can't drink. No wonder—he's broke.

She looks real nice in that new gown. She was not only just made for it, but for a fur coat, too.

She has a great sympathy for a lonely man—who needs someone to share a bank account with him.

Gossips

What she hears is never as exciting to her as what she overhears.

She takes people at their deface value.

Her favorite expression is: "I'm telling you this in confidence, because it was told to me in confidence."

You'll always find him at cocktail parties, where he drinks martinis, spears olives, stabs friends, and spills the beans.

You'll always find her in a beauty parlor, where she gets a faceful of mud and an earful of dirt.

She's never yet returned from the beach without a sunburned tongue.

She doesn't only engage in conversation—she syndicates it.

Tell most people something, and it goes in one ear and out the other. Tell her something, and it goes in both ears and out of her mouth.

She's very discriminating. She picks her friends—to pieces.

She knows how to guard a secret. She tells it to only one person at a time.

She weighs her friends' faults with her thumbs on the scale.

She's never happier than when she's taking someone for deride.

Sometimes she doesn't go into all the details. Her explanation is: "I've already told you more about it than I heard myself."

Time will never tell on her women friends as much as she does.

Recently she heard something about someone that she didn't repeat to anyone—she didn't know it was a secret.

The only two things that stop her from office-gossiping are the hands of the clock at 5:00 P.M.

She doesn't actually believe everything she hears—but that doesn't prevent her from repeating it.

She has gossip down to a fine art—she whispers it.

Her friends come to her parties with open throats and backs suitable for knifing.

One of these days she's going to get caught in her own mouth-trap.

His business is everybody's business.

He whitewashes himself by blackening others.

He never tells a lie—if the truth will do as much damage.

He must have goat glands—he's always butting in.

He'd have a few friends if he'd let opportunity do the knocking.

The only time he really gets interested in something is when he's sure it's none of his business.

His chief delight is giving you the low-down on the higher-ups.

Accustomed as he is to public peeking . . .

He's a professional athlete—of the tongue.

She was overheard breathlessly telling a friend: "I just must tell this before I find out that maybe it isn't true."

Her great fear is that if she doesn't gossip she'll have no friends to speak of.

She always listens to both sides of an argument—when it's by her next-door neighbors.

Watch out for her when she's in a train of thought—someone is about to get run down.

She's always flying around carrying her tale with her.

She has perfect gossip technique—she knows exactly how much to leave out of the conversation.

If she tended more to her knitting, she wouldn't get so tangled up in her yarns.

He should have been an elevator operator, the way he keeps running people down.

He can always be found at a cocktail party with a drink in one hand and a knife in the other.

In the business world he's known as the "meddle"-man.

He has the narrowest mind and the widest mouth.

It's easy to understand why he doesn't mind his own business —he doesn't have either a mind or a business.

He's been known to say: "And I can tell you all this without the slightest fear of verification."

He's the top man on the "quote-'em" pole.

He does all that knocking because he's never been able to ring the bell.

A bright eye may indicate curiosity; his black eye, too much.

She cultivates her friendships like a garden—with continuous little digs.

They call her "the Businesswoman." She's interested in business—everybody's.

Boy, can she turn an earful into a mouthful!

She's unhappy. She works in an office so big, it takes three days for one of her choice morsels of gossip to reach everybody.

One thing you've got to hand to her—she can put two and two together—whether they were or not.

With her a secret is either not worth keeping or "too good to keep."

Her gossip is enough to make everyone she-sick.

Her gossip is distilled wine from sour grapes.

Husbands

HENPECKED

He's underfed, undernourished, and over-wifed.

He wasn't born meek—he married her and got that way.

After all is said and done, it is she who has said it and he who has done it.

When they have an argument, they soon patch things up—his nose, his jaw, and his head.

They agree in their thinking—only she always has the first and deciding think.

The last time she said "yes" to him was when he proposed.

Before they were married, she promised to knit for him. Now she needles.

They once spent some time in a nudist camp; even there she told him what not to wear.

His big trouble is a superiority complex. The trouble is it belongs to her.

He really envies a bachelor who has to fix only one breakfast before he goes to work.

She has him on an allowance—fifty words a day.

He anticipated a peck of troubles when they were married, but not a hen-peck of troubles.

She's found a way to save on dishwashing time—she has him eating out of her hand.

In their home he puts his foot down—when she's through vacuuming under his chair.

She says she can read him like a book, but he wishes she didn't do it so loud.

Before they were married, he was an atheist and didn't believe in hell. However, she's now convinced him he was wrong.

He's a very efficient man-around-the-house. He knows the best time to take out the garbage—when she orders him to.

He bought a book, *How to Be the Boss in Your Own Home*, but she hasn't yet permitted him to read it.

He once asked a librarian, "Have you a book called *Man: the Master of the Home*?" She replied, "That must be in the Fiction Department, sir."

One thing is sure—any man would stay home with a wife like her. He'd have no choice—she has a double lock on the door.

When he proposed, he vowed he'd go through hell for her, and she's seeing to it that he keeps his promise.

He always takes her little hand in his—as she raises it to sock him.

When he isn't home she goes outdoors to insult the neighbors, just to keep in practice.

Once he decided to leave home, and he called up the zoo to find out whether they had an extra cage.

He walked out on her once, and she sneered: "You'll come back all right. How long do you imagine you'll be able to stand happiness?"

She keeps reminding him that when he proposed he vowed he'd die for her. All she wants to know now is how soon.

He's sorry now he put her on a pedestal. She can order him around better from that position.

He's so well trained, he feels in his pocket everytime he passes a mailbox.

He frequently has to phone her to say that he left his lunch money in his apron pocket.

He meets every matrimonial crisis with a firm hand—full of flowers and candy.

Marriage for him is like a railroad sign. When he first saw her, he stopped, then he looked—now he listens.

They have two cars, two TV sets, and two of many other things, but only one opinion—hers.

The only reason she promised at the altar to honor and obey him was that she didn't want to make a scene in front of all those nice wedding guests.

He should have suspected he was going to be henpecked when he hung the "Home, Sweet Home" plaque, and she snapped, "On the other wall, stupid!"

He should have known what he was in for when he carried her over the threshhold, and she commanded, "Wipe your shoes!"

He really should have been warned at the wedding reception when she tossed his bag of golf clubs from the top of the stairs.

He won her with soft soap; now he's washing the dishes.

Asked by the census taker what he did before he was married, he answered with a sigh, "Anything I wanted to."

His young son, studying geography, asked him, "What do you call those people who wear rings in their noses?" "Husbands," he replied.

When they were married, she promised to let him run the show, but forgot to add that she intended to write the script.

He's one husband who doesn't permit his wife to have her own way. She has it without his permission.

During their courtship he used to hold her hand and, ah! it was love. He's still doing it, but, oh! it's self-defense.

She doesn't always wear the pants in the family—sometimes she's satisfied with just a few cuffs.

When he asks her for a cup of hot chocolate, she gives him a chocolate candybar and a match.

She hires his office help. They're neither redheads nor blondes —they're bald and have mustaches.

Reincarnation really has him troubled. He's worried that if he comes back as a dog, she's sure to return as a flea.

In any argument with her, he's learned it's a bad idea to put his foot down—he's sure to get it stepped on.

He's satisfied to let her have the last word in an argument. Anything he says during one is the beginning of another argument.

Even when he hasn't said a word during one of her long tirades she's not satisfied—he has to wipe his opinion off his face.

He feels most at home at the race track, where it's nag, nag, nag.

His motto is: "A word to the wife is sufficient—just Yes."

After a poker session, he comes home and throws his arms right around her—before she can take a swing at him.

She's always glad to fix him a Bloody Mary—with *his* blood.

He's just been given three weeks to live—that's how long she's going to be away on vacation.

He's so henpecked, he'd have to ask her permission to kill himself.

He's the champion henpecked guy of all time. A year ago he got a Mexican divorce, and he still hasn't had the nerve to tell her.

THE BITTER HALF

There's only one thing that keeps her from being a happily married woman—him.

So far as she's concerned, he's one of the main reasons for twin beds.

She calls him "Hon"—Attila the "Hon."

Before they were married, he assured her that nothing was too good for her, and that's exactly what she's getting—nothing.

He's one guy who could make a wife a lucky widow.

When he proposed, he vowed their marriage would be for life. Now she wants to know why he doesn't show some.

She doesn't need a clock—she can tell the time by the length of his whiskers.

She keeps asking him to show her his birth certificate. She wants proof that he's alive.

She bought him an appropriate gift for their anniversary, something real timely and striking—an alarm clock.

He sleeps like such a dead one, she's already collected on his life insurance.

She was a career woman, and he told her at the start of their marriage that a career and marriage don't mix—so he's never worked.

She often tells him, "I do wish I'd known you when you were alive."

He likes to tinker around the house. In fact, she calls him the biggest tinker in town.

She's the power behind the drone.

He promised her a golden lyre when he proposed to her, and that's what she got—a golden liar.

She thought he was a bookworm, but soon learned that he was only a worm.

When the minister asked, "Is there anyone present who objects to this marriage?" she's sorry now she didn't say, "I do."

He vowed, when he proposed, that he would travel to the end of the world for her. Now she wishes he would, and that he'd stay there.

Ever since their wedding day she keeps asking, "When are you going to make me the happiest woman in the world—and leave me?"

She wishes she'd paid closer attention to the sign on the courthouse steps: "This way for marriage licenses. Watch your step."

Before their marriage, he told her he was unworthy of her. He should have kept it a secret—then it would have come as a complete surprise.

She has a bad case of matrimonial indigestion—something she married doesn't agree with her.

When he proposed, he asked her to say the words that would make her happy forever. Now she wishes she'd said, "Remain a bachelor."

He likes her in clinging dresses. The one she's wearing has been clinging to her for years.

She told him once she dreamed he had given her a mink coat. He generously said, "In your next dream wear it in good health."

She asked for a pearl necklace for her birthday, so he gave her a bushel of oysters and wished her luck.

She's money-mad. He never gives her any money—so she's mad.

She asked him for some money for a rainy day, so he gave her a rubber check.

He's hoping earnestly for a blessed event—her next raise in salary.

Right from the start he was determined to support her in the manner to which she was accustomed—letting her keep her job.

When they got married, he didn't expect her to give up her girlhood ways right away. He told her to go on taking an allowance from her father.

He always takes her to the best restaurants. Someday he may even take her inside.

She asked him for five dollars and he demanded: "What did you do with the five dollars I gave you yesterday—serial number B-6485291-F?"

She was his secretary and he married her because he didn't want to have to give her a raise.

She said she'd like to see the world, so he gave her a map.

When she complained that she'd had her fur coat for three years, he said, "That's not long—the animal had it for ten years."

He gets her all her jewelry from a famous millionaire—Woolworth.

She wears a diamond ring that reminds her of the capital of Arkansas—Little Rock.

He married her on $125 a week—*she* was earning it.

He got tired of hearing her complain that he never gave her anything, so he bought her a girdle and said, "Now, that should hold you."

She's had that fur coat so long, the Museum of Natural History is asking for it—they want to have it stuffed.

She says he's like a king to her—Henry the Eighth.

He tells her, "You're too extravagant. If anything happens to me, you'll probably have to beg." She says, "Oh, I'll get along —look at all the experience I've had."

She's wearing her wedding ring on the wrong finger—because she married the wrong man.

One of these days she's going to leave his bed—and bored.

She's sore at his family. When she told them he wanted to marry her, not one of them obpected.

He's a rarely faithful husband—very rarely.

He's surprised when anyone asks him if he cheats on his wife. "Who else?" he asks.

She's looking for a cook who can cook with one hand and hold him off with the other.

He's got a detective shadowing her. He wants to make sure he knows where she is when he's where he shouldn't be.

He never closes his eyes when he kisses—he has to be on the lookout for her.

She hasn't been speaking to him for quite a time—for quite a time he had with another woman.

They're carrying on a business together. She runs the business and he does the carrying on.

He's not worried about talking in his sleep. She and his girl friend have the same name.

He's really good at bringing home the bacon without spilling the beans.

It's been so long since he's made love to her, she wouldn't want him summoned if anything happened to her—he wouldn't be able to identify the body.

For him home is a place to go to, to raise a fuss because something went wrong at the office.

The only exercise he gets is being out seven nights running.

Drink makes him see double and feel single.

He's an indulgent husband—always indulging.

Too many bourbons on the rocks are putting their marriage there too.

He thinks home is where you go when all the bars close.

He leaves in the morning with a bundle of dough and comes home with a bun on.

When they met, she thought he'd make a good match. She didn't realize he'd always be lit.

In the morning, after one of his nights on the town, she asks: "How do you want your eggs—fried, scrambled, or intravenous?"

Asked if she cared to contribute something to the Home for Alcoholics, she said they could have him.

She's contemplating a divorce on the ground that he has alcoholic rheumatism—he gets stiff in every joint.

The way he tipsy-toes in late at night half shot, she's tempted to finish the job.

Just once she'd like to see him fix something around the house besides Manhattans and Martinis.

She keeps at a distance from him when she wears her leopard coat. With one deep 100-proof breath, he could change it right back to rabbit.

This is his third marriage—it seems he never loses an opportunity to make some woman miserable.

He tells her: "You don't deserve a man like me." She answers: "I don't deserve sinusitis either, but I've got it!"

Hypochondriacs

He's full of the joy of almost living.

His face is as long as a bankrupt undertaker's.

Her ailment is not so much chronic as chronicle.

She has a great talent for organ recitals—about those operations she's had.

Her life is a bed of neuroses.

He reads the obituary notices to cheer himself up.

She's constantly collecting ills and pills and getting chills.

He looks like a cheerleader for the morgue.

Being around him is like living in a pressure cooker with a stuck safety valve.

His usual greeting is "Good Moaning."

At the start of even a minor ailment she gets as hysterical as a tree full of chickens.

The way he groans and moans when he gets even a slight cold, you can't decide whether to call a doctor or a drama critic.

She has an indisposition that malingers on.

He's one of those rue-it-yourself experts.

118

Tell her how healthy she looks, and you've made a mortal enemy.

The inscription on his tombstone will undoubtedly read: *See!*

He not only expects the worst, but makes the worst of things when they happen.

She's one of those chronic invalids who have every ailment and disease described on television.

If an actor sneezes during a TV performance, she's sure she's caught cold.

He'll never shake anyone's hand if it's more than eighty degrees.

He's the kind of guy who goes to drive-in movies in an ambulance.

One of these days she's going to be *really* sick, and that will make her ecstatically happy.

She'll never feel better until the doctor tells her there's something wrong with her.

He must have been created for the benefit of doctors and psychiatrists.

No wonder he never has any rosy thoughts about the future— his mind is filled with the blues of the past and present.

He just quit his doctor. When he told him, "I have an awful pain every time I lift my arm," the doctor said, "So don't lift it."

He's very much against antibiotics since they've been found to cure some of his favorite diseases.

When nothing makes her sick, that's exactly what makes her sick.

One morning she woke up feeling real well, so she called the doctor to find out what was wrong with her.

He's one of those melancholy drinkers—every year is a good whine year.

When he has a sore throat he doesn't go to a doctor. He sits in front of his TV set with his mouth open so the actor playing the doctor's part can see his tonsils.

His wife says: "It's a damn shame the way he nurses a sham pain."

He doesn't look for pearls in oysters. Not he! He looks for ptomaine poisoning.

He's so high-strung, he should join the circus.

It's hard to tell, with all his complaints whether he's actually stricken or just chicken.

He's contemplating suicide, leaving a note reading: "I'm tired of being so damned happy."

Juvenile delinquents

The only sure cure for kids like him is birth control.

He's so tough, he's been turned down by every reform school in the country.

He's so tough, he makes his teacher stay after school.

The teacher asked him, "Who shot Lincoln?" and he snarled, "I don't squeal on nobody!"

He says he's a delinquent because he was repressed as a child. His parents punished him when he sawed the cat in half and gave his grandmother the hotfoot.

When he was eight years old, his parents pleaded with him to run away from home.

His parents almost lost him as a child. Unfortunately, they didn't take him far enough into the woods.

There's a kid who never fails to display his pest manners.

He's such a delinquent, he could go to reform school on a scholarship.

There's hardly a week when he doesn't come home from school with a note demanding a good excuse for his presence.

He hangs out in such a tough neighborhood that a cat with a tail is considered a tourist.

If he ever lives long enough to be an adult, it will be a remarkable tribute to his parents' and teachers' self-control.

He's given up one bad habit. He no longer smokes marijuanas during crap games.

His parents wish that birth control could be made retroactive.

It's too bad his parents didn't burn his britches behind him.

His parents don't give him all the allowance they can afford—they have to keep some back to bail him out.

He's 6 foot 3—until he gets a haircut; then he's 5 foot 7.

His folks spared the rod—and he's riding in it.

His parents were afraid to put their foot down, so now he steps on their toes.

He'd have been better off if his doting parents had been don't-ing parents.

His teachers have a good reason to spare the rod and spoil the child—they can't get the knife out of his hand.

The school psychologist advised the teacher: "You'll have to handle this boy carefully. Remember, you're dealing with a sensitive, high-strung little stinker."

He's real inventive. He took a fender from a Chevvy, the chrome from a Ford, the hubcaps from a Pontiac, and got—six months.

His parents gave him a motorcycle, hoping it would improve his behavior. All it did was to spread his meanness over a wider area.

Heredity is what makes parents of kids like him wonder about each other.

When he started off on the wrong track, his parents should have applied switching facilities.

Children can be a great comfort to parents in their old age—and this kid sure is helping his reach it faster.

Liars

You can tell when he's lying—if his lips are moving, he is.

On a recent safari, he encountered a bull and a tiger. He shot the tiger first. He figured he could shoot the bull anytime.

With him, truth is like a woman's girdle—it's made to be stretched.

They call her "Lilac"—she can lilac crazy.

He can never entirely murder the truth. He never gets close enough to it.

It's not so much that she exaggerates—she just remembers big.

She's almost truthful. She doesn't lie about anything except her age, her weight, and her husband's salary.

The way he handles the truth, he should work for the weather bureau.

He's the type who can make up his own bunk and then lie out of it.

Once he dislocated both shoulders describing the fish he caught.

Whether or not truth is stranger than fiction, in his case, in any event, it's scarcer.

123

He's the kind of fisherman who catches fish by the *tale*.

If he asks you to guess how much he made last year, you're safe in saying, "Half."

He says he enjoys a cold shower in the morning. He lies about other things too.

He's never been known to burn the candor at both ends.

His boss has received offers from four publishers for the fiction rights to his expense accounts.

You can believe half of what he tells you—the problem is, which half?

When his girl friend rejected him, he threatened to jump off a 300-foot cliff—but it was just a big bluff.

He's such a liar, when he has to feed his hogs, he has to get someone else to call them for him.

Testifying as a witness, he told a judge, "I have been wedded to the truth since infancy." Queried the judge: "Is the court to infer you are now a widower?"

When his conscience bothers him about something he's done to you, he'll come to you in a straightforward way—and lie about the whole thing.

He sadly, or badly, misuses the truth—which is the most charitable way of saying he's a liar.

He swears at himself after everything he says—he hates liars.

READING BETWEEN THE LYIN'S

I have to go to the mountains because of respiratory trouble. (*His creditors won't let him breathe.*)

I have hundreds of people under me. (*He's a watchman in a cemetery.*)

I dabble in oils. (*He's a gas station attendant.*)

My husband is a liver, brain, and lung specialist. (*He's a butcher.*)

I have a real big job. (*He washes elephants at the zoo.*)

The gowns I wear come from Paris. (*Paris, Kentucky.*)

My brother occupied a chair of applied electricity in a famous public institution. (*He went to the electric chair in Sing Sing.*)

My furniture goes back to Louis the 14th. (*It will, if Louis isn't paid before the 14th.*)

I got my fingers burned on Wall Street. (*He was picking up a lighted cigar from the sidewalk.*)

I have a big following. (*Five finance companies, 3 department stores, 4 landlords, and 7 collection agencies.*)

My ancestors go back as far as Columbus. (*Some of them even went as far as Chicago.*)

I hit the top in television. (*He fixes aerials.*)

I dine with the brass. (*No one would trust him with the silver.*)

No woman ever walks back when she goes for a ride with me. (*He drives a hearse.*)

My brother is a man of letters. (*He works in the Post Office.*)

Women are crazy about the way I kiss. (*They take one look at his face and exclaim, "What a kisser!"*)

I was a member of the underground. (*He was a conductor in the B.M.T.*)

I come from a family of standing. (*They're floorwalkers, elevator operators, and doormen.*)

I'm really clicking big around town. (*His dentures don't fit.*)

As a child, I was a musical prodigy. (*He played on the linoleum.*)

My father died before his time. (*They hanged him at 11:45 instead of midnight, as scheduled.*)

I'm doing settlement work. (*His creditors have finally caught up with him.*)

If I retired today, I'd have enough to live on for the rest of my life. (*. . . if he died tomorrow.*)

I had a hand recently in a big transportation deal. (*He thumbed his way across the country.*)

My dad was cleaned out in the 1929 stock market crash. (*A broker jumped out of the window and landed on his pushcart.*)

Losers

He's so fond of hard luck he runs halfway to meet it.

Just as he's about to make both ends meet, something breaks in the middle.

He had a fine job tramping on grapes to make wine—then he developed fallen arches.

He's the guy who always gets to the party after the liquor's run out.

He's as forlorn and neglected as Whistler's father.

He's one person who can buy artificial flowers and have them die on him.

His motto is: "Let a Smile Be Your Umbrella"—and he always gets a mouthful of rain.

He can always be counted on to do the right thing too late or the wrong thing too soon.

When he goes to the doctor to get a flu shot, it works real well—he gets the flu.

He's such a bumbler, when he gets to heaven he'll be sure to knock off one of the Pearly Gates.

He repaired his cuckoo clock; now it backs out and says, "What time is it?"

He bought a golf instruction book and followed its advice to keep his head down—and someone stole his golf cart.

No one is his equal at hitting the nail squarely on the thumb.

He even has to call in an interior decorator to change a typewriter ribbon.

He's standing on his own two feet—his car has been repossessed.

If he ever sold lighting fixtures, the sun wouldn't set.

Not only has he a hard row to hoe; he hasn't even got a hoe.

Lots of folks go through the School of Hard Knocks, but he's the one pupil who's sure to get hit on the head.

He was born with a silver spoon in his mouth. All the other kids had tongues.

He's the only person on record who used saccharine and got artificial diabetes.

He married a million-dollar baby, but after taxes she wasn't worth a dime.

In Las Vegas he even loses money on the stamp machine.

He plays cards and bets on the horses just for laughs. He's already laughed away his bank account and his car.

He bet on a horse that he was told would walk in. The only trouble was, the other horses ran.

He keeps putting bets on the horses' noses—he should bet on the legs.

When his bookie's place burned down, the only thing the firemen saved were his IOU's.

He bet on a sure-thing tip he got right from the horse's mouth —it turned out to be a horse laugh.

His life is like a razor—always in hot water or a scrape.

One thing has always kept him from making a fast buck—
a slow horse.

He comes up with a solution for every problem. It's always
practical, workable—and wrong.

Two business firms are fighting over his services—the loser
gets him.

He really has his ear to the ground—searching for his contact

He's a dependable person. You can always depend on him to
do the wrong thing.

He saved for years to buy an unbreakable, waterproof, shock-
proof watch—and lost it.

He bought a two-pants suit, and promptly burned a hole in
the jacket.

He's a real Don Juan with women—they *Don Juan* to have anything to do with him.

Not only is he not a Sir Galahad with women; he isn't even
a Sir Had-a-gal.

He dances as though he has two left feet—and also two right
ones.

All a girl has to do is agree to dance with him, and he's on
her feet in an instant.

When he trips the light fantastic, it may not be light, but it
sure is fantastic.

Lowbrows

He must be making a full-time career of coarseness and crudity. He couldn't be that good at it by accident.

His very presence holds you smell-bound.

He's a real baboon to society.

He says modestly that he's one of the common people. The fact is, you can't find anyone more common than he is.

Everyone has a real good word for him—they all whisper it.

He's such a lowbrow, his toupee is always slipping over his eyebrows.

He can't put his best foot forward without stepping on someone's toes.

He's the type who tells a woman her stockings are wrinkled—when she's not wearing any.

You can count on him to call a woman a cat instead of a kitten; a hen instead of a chicken; a goose instead of a duck; a sight instead of a vision.

If a woman asks him coyly if he can believe that she's 40, he's sure to say yes.

In the etiquette class he once attended, he was unanimously voted the student most likely to return.

He's real refined. He wears a T shirt to serve tea.

He likes to show off a picture of himself with a high-society friend. He's the one stepping on his cigarette so it won't burn his host's rug.

At every social event, he's the scent of attraction.

He's a stickler for etiquette. He knows which hand to use when tucking his napkin under his collar.

To show off his elegant manners, he holds a teacup with his pinkie sticking out—and the tea bag hanging from it.

Waiters are constantly offering to help him with the soup. From the sound, they think he might want to be dragged ashore.

It always did his dear mother's heart good to hear him eat.

You should see the sparks fly when he uses his knife and fork.

There's no denying that he has class—steerage.

He's an excellent illustration of the saying that age does not make a personage out of a person.

He's the type who keeps an elbow on each arm of his theatre seat.

He's as compatible with refined people as ham and matzohs.

If he ever finds himself out, he'll be the last one to do so.

He gets stabbing pains in his right eye every time he drinks tea. He should take the spoon out of the cup.

He never hurts anyone's feelings—unintentionally.

He's recently gone on a garlic diet. He lost a little weight and a lot of friends.

Once, studying some statistics, he said to his wife, "You know, every time I breathe, three Chinese die." She replied, "That doesn't surprise me."

He's the type who talks about rope to someone whose father was hanged.

He only opens his mouth to change feet.

He's a man with polish—on his shoes.

At his favorite night club, the tables are reserved. Too bad he isn't.

If he walked into a crematory he'd say, "What's cooking?"

He's a sportsman. When he spots an empty seat in a train or bus, he points it out to a lady—then he races her for it.

He prefers matches to a cigarette lighter. He can't pick his teeth with a lighter.

Years ago he was an amateur boxer, but he had to quit. He couldn't pick his teeth with the gloves on.

He's the economical type—he likes to save soap and water.

He recently said to his psychiatrist, "There's definitely something wrong with me—I keep getting this urge to take a bath."

He missed his vocation. He should be a garbage collector—he has that certain air about him.

That cheap aftershave stuff he uses stamps him as a guy with plenty of common scents.

He has a voice like a foghorn . . . like a buzz saw striking a rusty nail.

Never make the mistake of urging him to be himself—you couldn't give him worse advice.

Meanies

In any organization, he's the outstanding candidate for the Ways to Be Mean Committee.

He wouldn't dare eat his heart out—he'd break his teeth doing it.

Once a rattlesnake bit him. It was a terrible sight, watching it curl up and die.

He never hits a man when he's down—he kicks him.

He doesn't care what happens—so long as it happens to someone else.

He must have been raised on marble cake, brick ice cream, and rock candy.

Before firing an employee he gives him a raise, so he'll be losing a better job.

One night he dreamed he was dead—the heat woke him up.

He's the type who would steal the last fan from a fan dancer.

He once gave a blood transfusion to someone. The patient got double pneumonia from the shock of ice water in his veins.

When he visits a sick friend in the hospital he brings him some magazines, but advises: "If I were you, I wouldn't start any serials."

He always thinks twice before speaking, so he can come out with something really nasty.

There must be a lot of good left in him—none of it ever comes out.

He's the kind who'll borrow your pot and then cook your goose.

When it comes to helping someone, he stops at nothing.

There's nothing he wouldn't do for a friend, and he keeps it that way.

All his life he's followed the path of least assistance.

He rolls out the carpet for you one day, and pulls it out from under you the next.

So far as he's concerned, a friend in need is a friend to keep away from.

When you're in trouble, something is bound to turn up—his nose.

He'll never get dizzy from doing a good turn.

He's so cold-blooded, if a mosquito bit him it would die of pneumonia.

When he's finished with a mystery novel, he writes the name of the murderer on top of the first page before handing it on to his family.

He's never told his children that other families eat three meals a day.

He should buy fire instead of life insurance—there's no doubt where he's going.

His wife has to do her reading in the closet so his sleep won't be disturbed.

He's the type who can swim safely through shark-infested waters. He receives professional courtesy.

He once had a fight with a woman, and he would have won if she hadn't struck back with her crutches.

Muddleheads

He's so absent-minded, he went up to a horse at the race track and bet five dollars on a bookie.

He once fell down a flight of stairs. Landing at the bottom, he said, "I wonder what all that noise was about."

He keeps going around and around in a revolving door. He can't remember whether he's going in or coming out.

He kissed his wife good morning and said, "Take a letter, please."

He has three pairs of spectacles: one for near-sightedness, one for far-sightedness, and a third to look for the other two.

Once he attended a formal affair, properly attired in white tie and tails, and was the center of attraction. He should have worn pants too.

At a dinner party he was asked to pass his plate. He asked, "Which do you want—the upper or the lower?"

A nurse showed him the triplets his wife had just given birth to, and asked, "What do you think of them?" Absent-mindedly he said, "I'll take the one in the middle."

He bought a memory course, but never completed it. After the eighth lesson, he left the course in the subway.

He once left a note on his office door: "Back in an hour." When he got back he saw the sign, and sat down to wait.

When he told his doctor he couldn't remember things from one minute to the next, the doctor asked, "How long has this been going on?" He replied, "How long has what been going on?"

His wife asked him, "Do you remember me? I'm the woman you asked ten years ago to marry you." "Ah, yes," he answered, "and did you?"

He took up sculpture as a hobby, but had to give it up. Absentmindedly he kissed his model and chiseled on his wife.

An erroneous report of his death appeared in a newspaper, and he promptly sent himself a wreath.

Finding himself out in a pasture with a rope in his hand, he asked himself: "Now, have I found a rope or lost a horse?"

When a nurse informed him that he had just become the father of twins, he said, "Don't tell my wife. I want to surprise her."

He complained to a psychiatrist, "I'm always forgetting things. What shall I do?" The psychiatrist answered, "Pay me in advance."

He's so absent-minded, he kissed his wife goodbye and quarreled with his secretary when he got to his office.

At the Christmas office party he kissed his own wife.

Knowing how absent-minded he was, his family wired him a reminder while he was away from home: "Yom Kippur starts tomorrow." He wired back, "Put ten on the nose for me."

This guy is really absent-minded. He's a plumber—and when he answers a call he brings his tools with him.

Nudists

He's the camp's most absent-minded nudist. He went out one time with his clothes on.

There's a mutual attraction between her and a young man in the camp—they're in the nude for love.

She applied for the job as a guide in the camp—she enjoys showing visitors all over.

He's the camp's best golfer—he can go around the course in nothing.

He's the most handicapped fellow in the camp—he's near-sighted

She joined the nudist colony because she's interested in the naked facts of life.

She's a fine specimen of the nuder gender.

He joined the colony because he wanted to join a back-to-the-form movement.

She's indignant because the police are always breaking in, trying to get the goods on her.

She has the biggest problem of all the women in the camp—she's a bleached blonde.

He enjoys the colony's theme song: "Stares and Strips Forever."

As soon as he checked into the camp he demanded a room with sudden exposure.

He was attracted to the camp because of its name—Bearskin Lodge.

He brought his wife with him so they could air their differences.

Even in the nudist camp his shrewish wife tells him what not to wear.

He's a lawyer, and ever since he joined the colony he hasn't had a suit.

He has his eye on the most attractive female in the camp—he only wishes he could see her in a sweater.

The only thing she wears are beads—of perspiration.

She met a chap in camp, and it was a case of love at first sight —she knew exactly what she was getting.

She realizes now that nudism is only a skin game that attracts thousands of followers—mosquitoes.

He was nearly expelled from the camp because of a social error. He didn't look the president's wife in the eye when she was talking to him.

He's in danger of expulsion from the colony. He's always putting on airs.

He's a real snob—he comes down in the evening wearing a tie.

He misses his favorite game now that he's joined a nudist colony—strip poker.

His daughter won't join the camp until the day of her wedding—she wants to be married in white.

He became a nudist because he wanted to spend days without seeing a human face.

She'll always remember her first day in camp. It's like learning to fly—you never forget the first take-off.

Perfect pairs

They're well matched. He's a past master and she's a past mistress.

He's a pill and she's a headache.

She drives from the back seat and he cooks from the dining-room table.

She's 45 going on 37; he's 49 going on pep pills.

He's paunchy and she's punchy.

She's a rag, a bone, and a hank of hair; he's a brag, a groan, and a tank of air.

They get breakfast together. She makes the toast and he scrapes it.

He compares the bread she bakes with his mother's, and she compares his roll with her father's.

He's a has-been and she's a been-had.

It's a beef-stew marriage. She's always beefing and he's always stewed.

It's a nip-and-tuck marriage. He takes a nip, and she tucks him in.

It's a 50-50 marriage. She signs the checks; he signs the receipts.

It's a musical marriage. She's second fiddle, and he's drumming new romances.

It's a 50-50 marriage. She spends $50 for a hat and he spends 50¢ for a shirt.

They're a sparkling, shining couple. She sparkles with diamonds; he shines in his seven-year-old suit.

They're a fastidious couple. She's fast and he's hideous.

They get along perfectly. He never finds her in, and she's never found him out.

He phones to say he'll be late for dinner, and she's already left a note saying it's in the refrigerator.

She annoys him all day with her chattering, and he annoys her all night with his snoring.

They're madly in love—he with himself and she with herself.

They've got an exciting marriage. She pretends she's his secretary, and he pretends he's a misunderstood husband.

There's nothing he wouldn't do for her, and nothing she wouldn't do for him; in fact, they're devoted to doing nothing for each other.

They have so little in common, they don't even hate the same people.

They're so incompatible, they have nothing in common to fight about.

The only thing they have in common is that both of them are.

They're really well mated. They're inseparable and insufferable.

They're very class-conscious. They have no class and their neighbors are conscious of it.

They're going blissfully through life together—two minds without a single thought.

Playboys

He may not be a leader of men, but he sure is a follower of women.

He thinks life is very unfair—so many women and so little time.

The first thing he notices about a girl's looks is whether she looks available.

He's the principal reason why hotels have house detectives.

He's always doing the town, but he doesn't do it any good.

Give him one kiss, and it develops into a one-man crime wave.

Life for him is a matter of profits and lasses.

He counts sheep all night because he counts calves all days.

He admits that girls are a problem—but it's problems like that he enjoys wrestling with.

The apple of his eye is a little peach with the prettiest pair.

When he meets a girl, he doesn't care about having a clear field—he's got a nice, cozy den.

His park is worse than his bite.

He can be fairly well behaved once a girl gets to "no" him.

He's always AWOL—After Women Or Liquor.

When he gives a girl a present, he's well on the way to giving her a past.

He doesn't want to take a girl out and do things—he'd rather take her in and undo things.

When he gives a girl a string of pearls, the clasp is sure to go with it.

He's always ready to go to bat for a girl, if she has the right kind of curves.

He prefers to eat in restaurants where the dishes they serve aren't delicious, but the dishes that serve them are luscious.

He's frank and earnest with women. In Cleveland he's Frank and in Los Angeles he's Ernest.

His favorite game is called Photography. The idea is to put out the lights and see what develops.

He has two requirements for a girl—her pantry must be stocked and she must be stacked.

He knows how to handle girls who like a good time—often!

He attended a co-ed college where the girls went in for fact: and he went in for figures.

Girls go out with him by the dozens. They find it safer than going out with him alone.

He knows that love is blind, and he proves it by feeling his way around.

He's good at parlor tricks—especially slide of hand.

He's constantly in love instead of constant in love.

He prefers a girl who's sexy, not brainy. He says when he feels intellectual, there's always the public library.

He's tall, dark—and girls wish he were hands off.

He's a man of few words: Let's . . . Willya . . . Lemme.

He's a real playboy—he's constantly toying with sex.

He's gone around with more women than a revolving door in a supermarket.

When he pours a drink for a girl and says, "Say when!" he expects her to answer, "After this drink."

He doesn't believe a girl really understands a kiss until he has it from her own lips.

He's a guy who expects an "aye" for an eye.

So far as women are concerned, he's a perpetual-notion machine.

He's mastered the art of making a girl see the light when he has her in the dark.

He doesn't care at all about lengthening his days—he just likes to prolong his nights.

He's a man with no wife expectancy.

The only dates he's interested in are ones with no apron strings attached.

He has just one interest in life—himself.

He's a bachelor of arts. He's artful with women, yet has the art to stay a bachelor.

As a kid, he played Post Office. Now he plays Pony Express, because there's more horsing around.

One game he'll never play is Troth or Consequences.

He's a slick operator. He never gives a girl enough rope to make a marriage knot.

He's a gay dog, but he'll never be spousebroken.

He's the type who breaks off an engagement if the girl wants to go too far—like wanting to get married.

His stocks and bonds keep him in steaks and blondes.

He's losing his mind. He just received a letter warning him, "Stop playing around with my wife, or I'll kill you!" The letter's unsigned.

In the hospital recently, a shapely nurse held his wrist to check his impulse.

If he wants to keep his health, he'll have to lose some weight —about 120 pounds of blonde.

He's bored with his current girl friend. He's dating a female spiritualist to try out a new medium.

He knows a great deal about women—mostly from what he's been able to pick up.

He's a real fox—always manages to get what some wolf is after.

He doesn't care to share the best years of a woman's life— just her weekends.

Lots of women in town are urging him to take a memory-training course—so he can remember they're ladies.

Women are amazed at how well he dresses—and how quickly too.

He only goes out with girls who know all about the birds and the bees—and the pills.

He's the original Voice of Sexperience.

Girls are always running through his mind—they wouldn't dare walk.

He believes in love at first sight—it saves a lot of time.

He's had some awful temptations. It required all his strength and will power to yield to them.

People wonder who those women are they see him outwit.

He heard his clergyman say there are 358 sins. He's asking for the list—just in case he's missed something.

It's good that he isn't aware of a scientist's recent statement that no new sin has been discovered in the past 5000 years. It would give him an awful feeling of futility.

He's moving to a place out West where men are men and women are amenable.

His life is just a bed of ruses.

He keeps telling every girl that she has a beautiful figure. He can't seem to touch on some other subject.

The first thing he notices about an attractive woman is the size of her escort.

There have been many times when he decided to take a wife. His big problem has been whose wife to take.

While in Rome once, he picked up a little Italian. All she could say was "yes."

In the summer his car always seems to run out of gas. In the winter he takes girls for dog-sled rides and runs out of dog food.

Once he got beat up for kissing a bride—it was two years after the wedding ceremony.

He's very fond of his relatives, but of all his relations, he likes sex the best.

He doesn't think much of the old saying, "Beauty is only skin deep." He says that's deep enough for him—he's no cannibal.

He's fast going broke, not for a lack—but for a lass.

On an ice-skating rink recently he tried for hours to make a fancy figure, but got his face slapped.

He once got a black eye from a cough—coughing in a married woman's clothes closet.

He went around with a woman who had something that just simply knocked his eye out—her husband.

He needs a heart stimulant every night—a blonde or a redhead.

When he tells a girl he wants to be her good friend, he really means he wants to be good and friendly.

He's master of the art of setting a girl up in an apartment. He whispers a lot of suite things in her ears.

His convertible is called the "Mayflower"—quite a few puritans have come across in it.

He's glad to live in the U.S.A.—a great democracy, where a man has a choice of three governments: blonde, brunette, or redhead.

So far as he's concerned, America is the land of the spree and the home of the knave—the land of milk and honeys.

His favorite song is "I'll Be Seizing You in All the Old Familiar Places."

Girls may have trouble remembering his name or face, but they never forget his hands.

When he meets a girl, he starts to hem and paw.

He met a dazzler lately, and right away he was a different man—he gave her a fake name and address.

He took a girl to Florida to Tampa with her.

He's failing in business because he hasn't learned the difference between stocks and blondes.

He carefully considers the problem of pickups from every possible ankle.

He buys a girl a bikini and looks forward to seeing her beam with delight.

He has a lot of pet theories about women—chief among which is "Nothing succeeds like excess."

People always ask him, "Who was that dame you were obscene with last night?"

He has devoted the best leers of his life to women.

What a nightmare he had recently! He dreamed he was alone on a desert island with a dozen stunning girls—and he was a girl too!

They call him the "Dry Cleaner"—he works fast and leaves no ring.

The doctor advised him to cut out liquor and women, but he only cut out liquor. He says he can always drink when he's old.

He doesn't wear gloves when he goes out with a girl. He feels better without them.

He can read a woman like a book. What they object to is, he uses the Braille system.

The first thing he does is tell a girl she has "hidden charms" —then he starts hunting for them.

Women who go out with him think at first that he has a lot of culture, but they soon discover it's all *physical*.

He's very chivalrous—always wants to protect a girl from men who have ideas, because he has the same ideas himself.

It's not the high cost of living that's aging him prematurely; it's the high cost of loving.

He had a lot of money—but that was four blondes ago.

He never goes out with the NO-it-all type of girls.

The way he chases a skirt he's sure to wind up with a suit on his hands.

Chicks may have no terror for him, but the stork sure does.

His salary has been going to four figures—four shapely dames.

Once he decided to reform. The first week he cut out liquor. The second week, smoking. The third week he cut out women. The fourth week he was cutting out paper dolls.

THE PLAYBOY BOSS

As a boss, he's every pinch a gentleman.

His secretary is brushing up on her shorthand and typing—and also on her jiujitsu.

His father and he are carrying on a business together. His father runs the business—he does the carrying on.

He never paces up and down the office when he dictates—his secretary sits on his lap.

He likes to keep as busy as a bee at the office, with a little honey on his lap.

He has fired several secretaries because of mistakes they wouldn't make.

Seeing a shapely new stenographer pass his desk, he phoned his wife: "I'll be a little late tonight. A terrific sales campaign just occurred to me."

His secretary has just found something extra in her pay envelope—the key to his apartment.

He gasps for breath when he dictates to his current secretary —that girl can really run around a desk.

When he hires a secretary, he makes sure to tell her that there will be lots of opportunities for advances.

One girl in the office really has a great future. She's going places —with *him*.

He does his hiring not on the basis of grammar but of glamour.

He's always looking for a secretary who will come through in a pinch.

His idea of the perfect secretary is one who types fast and runs slow.

Although a bachelor, he listed a dependent son on his tax return. When a tax examiner commented, "This must be a stenographic error," he replied, "You're *telling me!*"

Playgirls

She's the kind of a girl you'd give your name to—but not your right name.

She's a home girl—she doesn't care whose.

There's a girl for you who leads a conventional life—she shows up at all the conventions.

She's the sort of girl you want very much to take home to Mother—when Mother isn't home.

Her boyfriend can't deny that she's given him the best weekends of her life.

Her conscience never no's what's wrong.

When it comes time at the altar for her to say "I do," she'll have to be careful not to come out with "I did."

The story of her popularity can be summed up in one word —yes.

She enjoys strip poker games. She shows the boys a thing or two—in fact, everything comes off just fine.

She's leading a delightful sexistence.

At college she was voted the Girl with Whom You Are Most Likely to Succeed.

She's a lover of the outdoors. She doesn't do so badly indoors, either.

Her motto is: To err is human, but it feels divine.

Asked how it happens that she has so many boyfriends interested in her, her answer is simple: "I give up."

She leads a simple, natural life. Her won'ts are few.

The way she dances, she doesn't know the difference between writhe and wrong.

She may not know how to cook, but she sure knows what's cooking.

She's an expert at giving the "Hail, fellow—we'll meet" look.

She owes that mink coat to her Power of Positive Winking.

"Always flirting" describes her to a tease.

Her "no" is like a comma—it doesn't mean a complete stop.

She was getting nowhere with the boys until she decided to get yeswhere.

The fellows all call her "Rumor"—she goes from mouth to mouth.

At college she wore a sweater with a letter given to those who made the team.

She knows how to raise a hem to get a him.

Good girls are born, but girls like her are made.

She's the real "goody-goody" type. When she's propositioned, she says, "Goody, goody!"

Her kiss speaks volumes—but it's far from a first edition.

She went to a bridge party recently, and was really enjoying it, until the cops looked under the bridge.

When she gets married, she should call her home "The Last Lap."

There are times when she's seen at a disadvantage—vertically.

She has a great capacity for love—so emotionally, so feelingly, so affectionately, and so universally.

Everyone thinks she's a Southern belle—she's so free and teasy on the drawl.

She tells bachelors, "Take it from me, don't get married."

She's climbing to success—lad by lad, and wrong by wrong.

She has had no difficulty keeping the wolf from the door—she invites him in.

Everyone knows her to be a lady in her own wrong.

Boy, is she experienced! When she kisses a guy, he knows he's been kissed—*she leaves a note.*

She frequents a bar where she just sits and watches the fellows come buy.

While she's waiting for the right man to come along, she's having a wonderful time with the wrong ones.

She's the answer to a playboy's prayer—to find the unbelievable—a passionate girl who is inconceivable.

The epitaph on her tombstone will undoubtedly read: *At Last She Sleeps—Alone.*

She's looking for a husband. Their wives wish she'd start with a single fellow.

Her old-fashioned mother used to go to the city and stop at the YWCA. *She* goes to the city and stops at nothing.

Her old-fashioned mother repulsed advances by taking to her heels. *She* advances the pulses of heels.

Her old-fashioned mother dropped a handkerchief to attract a man's attention. *She* wears it.

Her old-fashioned mother hurried home to do the dishes. *She* staggers home in her cups.

Her old-fashioned mother made her life a bed of roses. *She* makes her life a bed of roués.

Her old-fashioned mother dressed like Mother Hubbard. *She* dresses more like her cupboard.

She'll never make a good housewife. All she knows about lettuce is that it's a proposition.

She was being kept in a Park Avenue penthouse until recently. Her louse expired.

She's so knowledgeable about sex, the birds and bees study *her.*

Her taste in fellows has a uniform quality—soldiers, sailors, and marines.

She's kissed so many sailors, her lips move in and out with the tide.

She's not such a good dancer, but she can certainly intermission.

She's one for the book—every guy's little black book.

When she demurely asked a fellow, "Who said you can make love to me?" he answered, "Just about everybody."

She recently told a chap, "One false move—and I'll appreciate it."

Men don't meet her—she overtakes them.

She's learned that catching a man is like catching a fish— you've got to wiggle the bait.

Those baby stares of hers are for guys to trip on.

She flies occasionally from temptation, but makes sure to leave a forwarding address.

She doesn't chase men. Does a mousetrap have to chase a mouse?

It's amazing what she can get away with and still keep her amateur standing.

She's a real office cutie. She's not such a good typist or secretary, but the boss can always count on her in a clinch.

She can always get an advance from her boss out of petting cash.

Her boss treats her like a dog—a lap dog.

She was sitting in the lap of luxury until the boss's wife walked in unexpectedly.

On the line in the application blank headed "Sex," she wrote, "Once in a while."

In her latest job, when the boss said, "Let's sit down and get to work," she said, out of force of habit, "Which chair shall we sit in?"

In the office they call her the "Human Switchboard." When she walks across a room, all her lines are busy.

She can't even count on her fingers, but she sure can count on her legs and her hips.

Her boss hired her as his private secretary, but soon found she was a public stenographer.

SOMEONE'S PLAYGIRL DAUGHTER

She's only an astronaut's daughter, but she sure knows how to take off.

She's only an athlete's daughter, but she's always ready to play ball.

She's only a blacksmith's daughter, but she knows how to forge ahead.

She's only a bricklayer's daughter, but she certainly is well stacked.

She's only a butcher's daughter, but there isn't much more she can loin.

She's only a cab driver's daughter, but the fellows all think they auto meet her.

She's only a car dealer's daughter, but she sure has a swell chassis.

She's only a carpenter's daughter, but she knows every vise.

She's only a chimneysweep's daughter, but she soots all the fellows.

She's only a clergyman's daughter, but you can't put anything pastor.

She's only a coal dealer's daughter, but, oh, where's she bin?

She's only a columnist's daughter, but she's always chasing wild roomers.

She's only a communist's daughter, but all the boys get their share.

She's only a congressman's daughter, but she can sure fill a seat.

She's only a crapshooter's daughter, but she can roll you for all you have.

She's only a dairyman's daughter, but what a calf!

She's only a doctor's daughter, but, boy, can she operate!

She's only a draftsman's daughter, but she doesn't know where to draw the line.

She's only a dressmaker's daughter, but she knows how to keep the fellows on pins and needles.

She's only a farmer's daughter, but she sure knows her oats.

She's only an electrician's daughter, but she certainly has good connections.

She's only a fireman's daughter, but she's really going to blazes.

She's only a film censor's daughter, but she doesn't know when to cut it out.

She's only a fisherman's daughter, but the fellows all swallow her lines.

She's only a gardener's daughter, but she knows all the rakes.

She's only a globetrotter's daughter, but she manages to get around.

She's only an insurance broker's daughter, but the fellows like her policy.

She's only a milkman's daughter, but as a necker, she's the cream of the crop.

She's only a musician's daughter, but she knows all the bars in town.

She's only an optician's daughter, but with a couple of glasses she makes a spectacle of herself.

She's only a parson's daughter, but she has her following.

She's only a philanthropist's daughter, but she keeps giving things away.

She's only a photographer's daughter, but, boy, has she developed!

She's only a pitcher's daughter, but you should see her curves.

She's only a plumber's daughter, but she's making the most of her fixtures.

She's only a porch-climber's daughter, but you should see her stoop.

She's only a postmaster's daughter, but she sure knows her males.

She's only a prizefighter's daughter, but she knows all the ropes.

She's only a professor's daughter, but she can give the fellows a lesson.

Political acrobats

When he told his wife he'd been elected, she cried, "Honestly?" He answered, "Why bring that up?"

He chose politics as the most promising of all careers—and is he good at promises!

He's always throwing his hat in the ring. Too bad his head goes with it.

He can stand firmly in midair on both sides of an issue.

Biologists claim there isn't a perfect man on the entire globe. Apparently they haven't read his campaign literature.

Scientists claim that fog can now be made to order. This is hardly news to him.

He's very skilled at repairing his fences by hedging.

His latest campaign speech was interrupted thirty times by applesauce.

History repeats itself. In former days politicians dueled—he fences.

Around election time he can be depended on never to leave welfare enough alone.

He'd never run for office if he weren't paid by the year. He'd starve to death on piecework.

He'll stand for anything that will leave him sitting pretty.

He stumps his state both before and after election.

When he first ran for office, he appealed to the voters: "I never stole anything in my life. All I ask is a chance."

With someone like him in the legislature, we can understand why they have a chaplain there—to pray for the country.

He's opposed to a new bill requiring an intelligence test for candidates for public office. He complains that someone is always trying to destroy representative government.

There's a portrait of himself in his office, but it's not a true resemblance. He's shown with his hand in his pocket.

It's impossible to confront him with two issues so far apart that he can't straddle them.

He's mastered the 3 P's in politics—Promises, Promises, Promises.

It's untrue that there are 20,000 useless words in the English language. How else could he frame his political platform?

The planks in his platform that look so fine before election start warping very quickly afterward.

He had little to offer except an itch for office—and he was scratched at the polls.

He was defeated because he made a big mistake—he asked the voters to vote a straight ticket.

He told a friend he was defeated because of his youth. Said his friend, "But you're over sixty years and your youth is spent." Sadly he explained, "That's the trouble. They found out how I spent it."

He was elected because of his gift of gab, and was defeated because of his gift of grab.

Screwballs

He has a mechanical mind—too bad some of the screws are loose.

As a child he grew like a little acorn. Now he's come to maturity—he's a real nut.

When he goes to the zoo, he has to have two tickets—one to get in, one to get out.

You have to admit that fellows like him don't grow on trees —they swing from them.

He drinks psychopathic coffee—it's weak in the bean.

He has such a split personality, his psychiatrist told him to go chase himself.

He has such a split personality that his psychiatrist sends him two bills for each visit.

He needs a checkup from the neck up.

His new apartment has made him happier—it has wall-to-wall padding.

Before his first session with a psychiatrist was over, the psychiatrist got on the couch.

Offering candy to his girl friend, he said, "Sweets to the sweet." She thanked him and asked "Won't you have some of these nuts?"

He's so crazy about baseball, he never dreams about girls. He's afraid he'll lose his turn at bat.

He calls his brother up every night—and his brother doesn't have a phone.

Four psychiatrists have yet to find out what makes him tick—and especially what makes him chime on the hour and half-hour.

He keeps hitting home runs in his head—he has bats in his belfry.

No wonder he flies off the handle—he has a screw loose.

He's going around with a woman who's cross-eyed, knock-kneed, buck-toothed, and with an awful figure—but what lovely nightmares she has!

In one way he's fortunate. He could go completely out of his mind, and no one would know the difference.

He goes from psychiatrist to psychiatrist, always ready to sign for treatments on the dotted couch.

He's been taking so many tranquilizers he no longer worries about paying his psychiatrist's bills.

His case is one that's enriching medical and psychiatric science. He's already paid two brain specialists and four psychiatrists more than $5000 each.

He started with psychiatric treatment slightly cracked. He's finishing up completely broke.

The sign in his psychiatrist's waiting room reads: Worry Now, Pay Later.

He's been going to a psychiatrist to be cured of alcoholism. It's costing him so much, he soon won't be able to afford liquor.

When a psychiatrist told him: "Congratulations! I've cured you of your delusion," he answered unhappily, "So what? Yesterday I was Napoleon—today I'm nobody."

He's girl-crazy. Girls won't go out with him—that's why he's crazy.

Show-oafs

He has such a big mouth, he can eat a banana sideways, or sing duets by himself.

He's like a Christmas tie—loud and useless.

When they go to a party, his wife warns him, "Remember, when the party is over, be sure to go up to the host and apologize."

At almost every party, his wife is sure to be asked by someone, "What does your husband want to be when he grows up?"

They call him the "Mastoid of Ceremonies"—he's a pain in the ear.

He claims he lives by his wits. It's remarkable how a person can live on so little capital.

His wisecracks are always greeted with a tremendous burst of silence.

When he leaves a party, the guests know the meaning of comic relief.

He won't have to wait till he dies to be at his wit's end.

He thinks he's a born wit—he sure must have lost a lot of ground ever since.

He thinks he's a real funnyman, but he couldn't even entertain a doubt.

He thinks the world will beat a path to his door because he's built a better claptrap.

A monkey took one look at him and yelled, "To heck with the Darwin theory—they're not going to make a man out of *me!*"

He has a cute hobby that burns his friends—hotfoots.

He's perfecting waterproof matches so he can even give hotfoots on rainy days.

His idea of a practical joke is to go into a Home for the Blind and flatten out the Braille.

He's driven a dozen friends crazy by sending them wires reading "IGNORE FIRST WIRE."

He has a well-earned reputation as the death of the party.

Pandemonium doesn't merely reign when he's around—it pours.

There are people who are liked wherever they go—he's only liked whenever he goes.

He claims he lives by his wits—that accounts for that half-starved look on his face.

If you want to see unmatched technique, just watch him making a fool of himself.

As the "life of the party," he needs more effective gags—right across the mouth.

There are people who meet him who never forget a face; in his case they're willing to make an exception.

He has a waterproof voice—no one can drown it out.

He's a live-wire—wired mostly for sound.

There was a minute at one party when a guest didn't recognize him. It was the most enjoyable minute the man had ever spent.

There's something about him at social gatherings that definitely attracts women—to other men.

Success hasn't gone to his head—just to his mouth.

He's short of horsepower and long on exhaust.

He's such a braggart, if he can't boast about knowing something, then he boasts about *not knowing it*.

Every year he takes a boast-to-boast tour.

Listening to him makes you think of a river—small at the head and big at the mouth.

He says he'd only marry a girl who can take a joke—that's the only kind who would take him.

At any party he attends, all that the guests want is a place to hang their hats and *him*.

Just encourage him, and you'll be slain by the jawbone of an ass.

He comes into a room shooting from the lip. He wants to hold you spielbound.

He's always out to have the time of your wife at a party.

The surest way to check this "life of the party" is to let him pick up the check.

Snobs

She's so ritzy, she has alligator bags under her eyes.

She won't eat a hot dog unless it's been certified and warranted by the kennel club.

He's proof that stuffed shirts come in all sizes.

He's such a snob, he refuses to work until the government gives him an unlisted Social Security number.

His son has gone into the army, and he's applied for an unlisted serial number for him.

As society swells, he and his wife are the mold on the upper crust.

They don't say that their ancestors came over on the Mayflower. They insist that they had their own boat.

They've moved to Snuburbia.

They can trace their family tree back to the time when their family lived in it.

They even have monogrammed tea bags.

They have a home in a nice location—on the outskirts of their income.

They're buying a home in a restricted development, where no one is permitted to build a house they can afford.

163

They're trying to keep up with the Joneses, and the bill collectors are trying to keep up with them.

They're moving to an exclusive neighborhood—where the rents are high and the noses are higher.

They can look down on other people, but only because they're living on a bluff.

He's full of rectitude, platitude, and high-hatitude.

He deliberately broke a leg skiing. He wanted a status symbol.

The only thing he ever did was inherit an old family tax loophole.

He wants to know only the people who don't want to know him.

When the doctor was about to give his wife a local anesthetic, he demanded, "Doc, give her the best—*something imported.*"

He looks like something that was stuffed by a good taxidermist.

She holds her head high—too bad she doesn't keep her nose on a friendly level.

She mightn't have such a wrong slant on things if she stopped looking down her nose.

She's as snippy as she's hippy.

She has two nose specialists—one for each nostril.

Tightwads

He's the type who takes things for gratis.

He's a real carefree guy—doesn't care as long as it's free.

Money means nothing to him. When you ask him for some, you get nothing.

All his clothes are tailored with one-way pockets.

He's a strict believer in free speech—like using friends' phones for long-distance calls.

He weighs 175—135 without his money belt.

Amazing how he always manages to be away from the table when the waiter brings the check. No wonder they call him the "After-dinner Sneaker."

He isn't particular how people treat him—just so long as they do.

He's made an art of not picking up the check. You've really got to hand it to him.

He's well known as a dollar-a-year man—it's all he ever spends.

He's just had his dentures tightened so he can put a better bite on his friends.

The longest trip known to mankind is the one his hand takes to his pocket.

Comes December, and he starts dreaming of a tight Christmas.

He's one of those free-loaders who's known from host to host.

He does crossword puzzles vertically so he won't have to come across.

His idea of an enjoyable vacation is to stay at home and let his mind wander.

He saves a lot of money on vacations. He keeps cool all summer by sponging.

He's a man of rare gifts—it's rare when he gives one.

When he donates money to charity, he likes to remain anonymous—so he doesn't sign his name to the check.

He doesn't believe in the popular slogan "Give till it hurts,' but he always yells "Ouch!" when he's approached for a donation

His automobile is so old, his car insurance policy covers theft, fire, and Indian raids.

He's one of those tightwad playboys who tries to make every dollar go as far as possible—and every girl too.

A woman just returned his ring. The envelope was marked "GLASS—HANDLE WITH CARE."

He doesn't always insist that the girl pay the dinner check. He sometimes offers to flip her for it.

When he's out with a girl he has plenty of savoir-faire, but no taxi fare.

He's very unhappy. He's had Blue Cross insurance four years, and hasn't been sick once.

The best definition of an optimist: One who tries to borrow money from guys like him.

An optimist is one who makes the mistake of lighting a match before asking him for a cigarette.

He's one of those two-fisted spenders—both tightly closed.

One of his employees came in a hour early each day for a month, and he charged him rent.

He has people working for him twenty years without ever having asked for a raise—that's why they've been there twenty years.

He's determined not to go without taking it with him; he's bought himself a fireproof money belt.

He even has a burglar alarm on his garbage can.

He recently bought some shirts cheap and changed his name to fit the monogram.

He's the kind who can't be ordered around—unless its a round of whiskey.

His girl asked him for a book of poetry, so he went to a bookstore and asked for a volume of free verse.

He's waiting for a total eclipse of the sun so he can send a night-rate telegram.

The way he nurses a drink it looks like he's drinking from an hourglass.

At his own cocktail parties the whiskey flows like glue.

Of all the near-relatives in the family he's the closest.

When his kids want ice cream because they feel warm, he tells them ghost stories to make their blood run cold.

No one can find fault with his cleanliness. He's been sponging for years.

It's reached a point where he won't even spend the time of day

He's widely recognized as a man who gives no quarter. Waiters, bellboys and taxi drivers can testify to that.

When he takes a dollar bill out of his pocket, George Washington blinks at the light.

He can make a nickel go so far, the buffalo gets sore feet.

Wet blankets

It's people like him that make you long for the solitary life.

A few minutes with him makes you want to jump for joy—off a tall building.

He's known everywhere as a VIB—a Very Insistent Bore.

When it's time for him to get up and go home, he's full of get-up-and-stay.

He's the kind you bid a welcome adieu.

There are three ways of saying goodbye to him: Adieu, Adios, and Arsenic.

One thing you can expect from him in abundance—and that's redundance.

He claims he can imitate any bird. He's apparently overlooked the homing pigeon.

He's a person who's going places—and the sooner, the better.

He holds people openmouthed with his conversations. They can't stop yawning.

You can always spot him at a cocktail party. He has a highball in one hand and someone's lapel in the other.

He's just what the doctor ordered—a pill.

He's only dull and uninteresting until you get to know him. After that, he's just plain boring.

He's such a bore, he even bores you to death when he's complimenting you.

His stories always have a happy ending. Everyone is delighted when they finally end.

He's so dull, even his dog got bored and left him.

He's good for people's health. When they see him coming, they take long walks.

He umphasizes every other word.

He always has a flood of words and a drought of ideas.

It's not bad enough that he explains everything—he even explains his explanations.

He has his tongue in your ear and his faith in your patience.

He always has a couple of hours to spare, and is constantly on the lookout for someone who hasn't.

The real problem of having leisure time is to keep him from using it.

He can dive deeper into a subject than anyone you've ever known. The trouble is, he stays under longer and comes up drier.

It's true that he's a man of few words. The trouble is, he keeps repeating them.

No one can equal his genius for squeezing a minimum of thought into a maximum of verbiage.

There's one thing that can be said in his favor: it requires no small talent to be as unbearable a bore as he is.

He doesn't need to repeat himself. He gets it trite the first time.

He's a monologist who becomes a monopologist until you become a moanologist.

He serves one useful purpose. Running away from him is the only exercise some of his acquaintances get.

All he has to do is open his mouth, and his foot falls out.

So far as his sense of humor is concerned, he's living on the wrong side of the cracks.

By the silence in the room, you can safely conclude that he has just told a joke.

Some people provide happiness wherever they go; he, whenever he goes.

He's like a summer cold—you just can't get rid of him.

He has occasional flashes of silence that make his conversation brilliant.

His parties are so dull that a guest who dropped dead at one was the life of the party.

One advantage of going to his dreary parties is that you can get home at a decent hour.

On leaving one of his parties, a guest usually says, "I've had a most enjoyable evening. Sorry this wasn't it."

He says he'd go to the end of the earth for his friends. They only wish he would, and that he'd remain there.

Encountering three guests strolling together at a resort hotel, he asked, "What's going on?" "We are," they chorused—and did.

It's not that he doesn't know how to say nothing. The trouble is, he doesn't know when.

If he should remark, "There's something I've been intending to say, but I just can't seem to think of it," be sure to suggest, "Probably an appointment you're already late for?"

Even as a child, he was such an insufferable bore that when he was nine years old his parents ran away from home.

"Please don't bother seeing me to the door," he said to a weary host. "It's no bother," was the answer. "It's a real pleasure."

Wives

BABBLERS

In his entire life he never spoke as fast as when he proposed. He must have sensed it was his last chance to do any talking.

She speaks 140 words a minute, with gusts up to 180.

The one and only time she stops talking is when her mother starts.

He murmured as he sat at the dinner table, "How tranquil it must have been in the Tower of Babel!"

He married her because of her beautiful mouth. He wishes now she wouldn't keep it open so much.

When he goes to a dentist, he has her alongside the chair babbling away, so he won't feel any extra pain.

It's no help to him when she lets her mind go blank—she neglects to turn off the sound.

A doctor told them he needed rest and quiet, and prescribed a tranquilizer—to be taken by her.

She says, "I just don't understand my husband. He hardly ever talks, unless he has something to say!"

Out on a golf course with her once, he found a trap on the course that was exasperating—she just wouldn't close it.

She asked the doctor to look at her tongue to see if it was coated. He shrugged, "No need to—you never find grass on a racetrack."

They've been married fifteen years, and he loves her still.

He'd be willing to forget the fact that she set her trap for him when they first met—if she'd just shut it now.

He wouldn't object to her having the last word—if she'd only get to it.

Queried by one of those radio-survey phone calls, "To whom are you listening?" he replies, "To my wife—who else?"

In any argument with her he always gives in. What's the use? —it's just his word against thousands of hers.

He knows now why Adam was created first—to give him a chance to say something.

He's just phoned the doctor: "My wife has dislocated her jaw. If you happen to pass by in a week or so, you might drop in— no hurry."

He's an outstanding linguist. He's mastered many tongues but not hers.

At bedtime, when she asks, "Is everything shut up for the night?" he patiently replies, "Everything else, dear."

He understands why she got that double chin—too much work for one.

Once she rebuked him: "What's the idea? You yawned seven times while I was talking to you." "I didn't," he said. "I was just trying to say something."

From the day they were married he hasn't been on speaking terms with her—only on listening terms.

On their latest anniversary she asked, "Can't we celebrate?" He was tempted to reply, "Yes, let's have two minutes of silence!"

The only time she never interrupts him is when he talks in his sleep.

THE BALL AND CHAIN

Before he married her, he thought she was a shrinking violet. Now he knows the word should be "shrieking."

He wishes she were his mother—so he could run away from home.

She's a bridge fiend. Only a fiend could kick as hard as she does.

She claims they're happily married. The fact is, *she's* happy, *he's* married.

He should have been warned when he attended the funeral of her first husband—the corpse had such a relieved look.

When he agreed to marry her, it was a load off his chest—her father and two husky brothers got off it.

He was really fooled when he asked her to marry him and she said she was agreeable.

When he complains that she's driving him to his grave, she sneers, "What did you expect to do, walk?"

When she told him the man who married her would get a prize, he should have asked for a look at it first.

During their courtship she purred that she was saving herself for him. Now he wants to know why, at 165 pounds, she has to save so much.

Before they were married, her chin was her best feature—now it's a double feature.

She's resorted to henna, and he's resigned to Gehenna.

He doesn't have to worry about making a fool of himself—she's doing the job for him.

She's the beneficiary of his $100,000 insurance policy, and she wants to know what excuse he can give her for living.

He recently wired a hotel to reserve "a suitable room where I can put up with my wife."

He well remembers the night, five years ago, when he had a wreck in his car—he's sorry he married her.

A friend told him, "I just got a cute little poodle for my wife." He sighs, "I wish I could make a trade like that!"

He recently phoned his boss to say he couldn't report for work because his wife broke an arm—his.

For his last birthday she gave him a present that really made his eyes pop out—a shirt with a collar two sizes too small.

She sneers, "I had to marry you to find out how stupid you are." He replies, "You should have known that the minute I asked you."

She often berates him: "Before we were married, you told me you were well off." He answers, "I was, and didn't know it."

Once she screamed, "I should have taken my mother's advice and never married you. How she tried to stop me!" "Holy mackerel," he exclaimed, "how I've misjudged that woman!"

There's no doubt who's the boss in their house—she's taken complete charge of the controls on the electric blanket.

He's often asked why he has that number F-83659 tattooed on his back, and he explains: "That's not a tattoo—that's where my wife ran into me when I opened the garage door."

He came home one night, and found his partner making love to his wife. Amazed and dumfounded, he said, "Herman, I must —but you?"

She recently asked an insurance agent: "If I take out a $500,000 insurance policy on my husband's life and he should die the next day, what would I get?" He answered, "Life."

His daughter, hesitating to accept a proposal, told him, "Dad, I hate to leave mother." "That's all right, dear," he said, "just take her with you."

He says that drink is the curse of his marriage. Once it made him shoot at her—it also made him miss.

He sued for a separation, but in court she denied that they weren't getting along very well together. "We did have an argument, judge, and I shot him," she said, "but that's as far as it went."

He was recently run over by a hit-and-run driver. When a cop asked him if he'd gotten the car's plate number, he said, "No, but I'd recognize my wife's laugh anywhere."

He's getting a little leery—she's just bought him a deerskin coat to wear on his next hunting trip.

She read his fortune on a weight card: "It says you're magnetic, a born leader, and widely recognized for your strength of character—it's got your weight wrong, too!"

THE GETTER HALF

He took her for better or worse. She took him for everything.

The outcome of their marriage depends on his income.

She's really his "better half." When she asks him for money, he'd better have it.

She loves him for what he is—well-to-do.

He always has a voice in what she buys—the invoice.

On his birthdays she always sends him a card reading "Money Happy Returns."

They have a joint bank account. It's in two names—her married name and her maiden name.

She runs up expenses so fast it leaves him breathless.

She's his treasure so long as he remains her treasury.

Running a house is a matter of checks and balances. The more checks she writes, the worse his balance gets.

She'll get back that warm feeling for him—when he buys her a fur coat.

There's one thing about him that she loves—he wonders how long it will take her to spend it.

He keeps a goldfish bowl on his desk. He likes to see something opening its mouth without asking for money.

When he leaves for a business trip, she wheedles, "Be sure to write—even if it's only a check."

She's worried about his insomnia—she hasn't been able to go through his pockets for months.

He tells her he can't face those bills she's run up. She says, "You don't have to face them—just foot them."

Instead of sending his suits to the cleaner, she industriously removes the spots herself—five spots, ten spots . . . .

She was his secretary before they were married; now she's the treasurer.

Their ship of matrimony isn't moving so smoothly, because she won't stay away from the sales.

He's convinced there's no life on the moon. There are no charges for calls there on her phone bills.

The things she buys all the time for the house makes him realize how few things it lacks.

She was determined to marry a man clever enough to make a lot of money, and dumb enough to spend it all on her.

She's disturbed because lately she can't seem to balance her budget. According to her figures, she's spending less than he's earning.

He keeps reminding her, "Any day now we're liable to be on a pay-as-you-went basis."

There's no doubt she knows how to make a dollar go far—so far that he never sees it again.

When he proposed, he declared, "I'd go through anything and everything for you." So far, he's only gone through his bank account.

The gag about the absent-minded husband who sent his wife to the bank and kissed his money goodbye doesn't apply to him. It isn't absent-mindedness in his case—it's a fact.

He doesn't worry when she isn't at home for several days—where else would she be but shopping?

A friend told him, "My wife dreamed last night she was married to a multimillionaire." "You're lucky," he sighs, "My wife has that dream in the daytime!"

They both like the same thing. The trouble is, he'd like to hold on to it and she likes to spend it.

She calls him a "good egg"—sure, but wait till he's busted.

He'd better hang on to his capital if he doesn't want her to lose interest.

Once he told her he might be going broke. "Don't worry, dear," she said, "I'll always love you even though I'll never see you again."

On the verge of bankruptcy one time, he asked a friend to break the news to her gently. "Tell her I'm dead," he suggested.

He gave her the world with a fence around it, and she turned around and gave him the gate.

HOUSEKEEPERS

The meals she cooks are putting color in her husband's face —purple.

When it comes to housekeeping, she likes to do nothing better.

She's had him on frozen food so long, his stomach is sending out blizzard warnings.

He's provided her with a modern kitchen—now all he needs in it is an old-fashioned wife.

She doesn't have to hire domestic help—she seems to have married it.

If death ever approaches, his final wish will be for her to cook his last meal—then he'll feel more like dying.

Where there's smoke, there she is—cooking.

She smothers the steak in onions, but it still tastes as if it died a hard death.

What a cook! She's burned so many slices of bread that their toaster has been declared a fire hazard.

One time she purred: "Dear, what will I get if I cook another dinner like tonight's?" He answered, "My life insurance!"

She feeds him so much fish, he's breathing through his cheeks.

Her cooking is really something to write home about—for his mother's recipes.

He's her second husband. She keeps wanting him to eat everything her first husband did—but he refuses to commit suicide.

He deserves a decoration for eating one of her meals—a purple heartburn.

His is a real surprise marriage. When he comes home to a well-cooked meal and kind words, boy, is he surprised!

She says she's too weak for housework. He's not strong either for her idea of housework.

When they met she told him she'd been to a cooking school —he thinks she must have learned in ten greasy lessons.

He sure knows how to settle her hash—with bicarbonate.

It always amazes him that she's able to see right through him when she can't see a button missing from his coat.

Right after marriage, she decided what to do to have soft, white hands—NOTHING.

She gets mad when he says the soup is cold. Indignantly she asks, "What do you want me to do—burn my thumb?"

All she knows about cooking is how to bring him to a boil.

Before marriage she turned his head with her charm—now she turns his stomach with her cooking.

She serves him blended coffee—today's and yesterday's.

There are enough grounds in his coffee cup for a divorce.

Ever since their marriage, they've gone through thick and thin. When it comes to cooking, she's thick and he's thin.

One night she whispered, "there's a burglar in the kitchen. He's eating the casserole we had for dinner." He said, "Go back to sleep—I'll bury him in the morning."

She's not a cook—she's an arsonist.

Since their marriage, he's learned a great deal about reincarnation—only they call it hash.

Some wives can cook but don't. His wife can't cook but does.

She has one fixed theory in the kitchen—if it doesn't move, wrap it in aluminum foil.

Once she cried, "The dog ate the meatloaf I made for you." He said, "Stop crying. I'll buy you another dog."

He no longer gets his morning dish of instant oatmeal—she lost the recipe.

When he pleads to be surprised for dinner, she obliges—she soaks the labels off the cans.

He's had all he can bear of her cooking—he's threatening to go home to her mother.

She's served him so many TV dinners, he's thinking of looking for a new sponsor.

When she tells him, "Woman's work is never done," he counters, "That's right—and your housekeeping proves it."

Her kitchen is so messy and cluttered, when bread pops out of the toaster, he'd be late for work if he tried to find it.

Is she lazy? He defies anyone to produce another housewife who washes dishes in bed.

He married her because he wanted someone to cook and keep house. Trouble is, she married *him* for the same reason.

He's given up asking her to straighten up the house. She wisecracks, "Why—is it tilted?"

He always has the last word with her—in the mornings anyway. He says, "Oh, don't get up. I'll have breakfast downtown."

Sometimes she tells him she has a marvelous meal planned for him. "I'll tell you about it on the way to the restaurant," she says.

She's really a terrific housekeeper. She's been divorced three times, and in every settlement she keeps the house.

STRAYERS

She's happily married—her latest boyfriend likes her husband.

One time while he was on vacation, she wrote him: "Now be sure to go out with no one but men, and I'll do the same here back home."

She insists that at the bottom of her heart she loves her husband—there's a boyfriend at the top.

WIVES : : 181

Even after ten years of marriage her husband finds her entertaining—when he comes home unexpectedly.

She was told by a fortuneteller, "You should be happy—a nicer man than your husband you have yet to meet." She replied, "How exciting! When?"

She married him for his money. Now all she's interested in is a little change.

Accused of having been seen with another man, she protested, "Dearie, it was only my husband—you know there's no one but you!"

A friend said, "Your husband is brilliant-looking. I suppose he knows everything." She replied, "Don't be silly. He doesn't even suspect."

She frequently boasts about the "straight and narrow." She's undoubtedly referring to her girdle.

She's the type who considers herself too good to be true.

Once her husband caught a man embracing her, and he yelled, "Now I know everything!" "Oh, yeah?" she sneered. . . . "When was the Battle of Vicksburg?"

Teaching his young son to count, he asked, "What comes after 10?" Answered the kid, "The man next door."

Writers

He's putting everything he knows into his next literary work. It's sure to be a short story.

It's a first-grade novel. The only trouble is, most readers have gone beyond the first grade.

You can read yourself to sleep with his novel—it's a great yawn.

He should have put a finishing touch to that story—a match.

He must have written that play on a tripewriter.

His book is bound to be a Best Smeller.

In writing it he must have used a dictaphony.

His books will be read long after Shakespeare, Dickens, Hemingway, and Faulkner are forgotten—but not until then.

Reading his novel is like eating an artichoke—you have to go through so much to get so little.

As a mystery novel, it's just run-of-the-morgue.

He claims he reaches thousands of readers—good thing they can't reach him.

They call him the "Pharmacist." Every book he writes is a drug on the market.

His preface states that the characters bear no resemblance to any person living or dead. That's precisely what's wrong with it.

He claims he puts fire into his writings. He'd be better off to put his writings into the fire.

He's just written something that will be accepted by any magazine—a check for a year's subscription.

He's taken up writing as a career and has already sold several things—his watch, typewriter, overcoat, and furniture.

"The play of the future" is what he calls his latest brain child. Another like it, and he won't have any future.

No fewer than five characters die in his mystery novel and are interred in the plot.

The story has as much action as a snake's hips.

His novel is an indefinite idea in infinite ink.

His novel should win a Pulitzer prize—at least the first two letters.

The book will leave its mark on literature—like chicken pox.

He wanted to be a novelist badly, and he's achieved his ambition—he's a bad novelist.

He writes books nobody will read, and checks nobody will cash.

He's one author who's sure to be flooded with pan mail.

Nicknames

They call him ACCORDIONIST: He plays both ends against the middle.

They call her AFTER-DINNER SPEAKER: If she speaks to you, she's after a dinner.

They call her ANGEL: She's always up in the air, harping about something.

They call her ARCHER: She knows how to keep her beaus in a quiver.

They call him BEAN: Everyone strings him along.

They call him BIOLOGIST: He crosses an intersection with a convertible and gets a blonde.

They call her BOTTLENECK: If a fellow opens a bottle, she's ready to neck.

They call her BUSINESS WOMAN: She's interested in everybody's business.

They call him BUTTON: He's always popping off at the wrong time.

They call him CAESAR: He's a man of great nerve and wonderful Gaul.

They call him CATERPILLAR: He got where he is by crawling.

They call him CHARACTER ACTOR: When he shows any character he's acting.

They call her CHEWING GUM: She's Wrigley all over.

They call her CHORUS GIRL: She's always kicking.

They call him CLASS-CONSCIOUS: He has no class, and everyone is conscious of it.

They call him CLIFF: He's a big bluff.

They call him CLOCK: His hands are always moving over figures; they go around girls so fast, it alarms them.

They call him COLD: You can't get rid of him in a hurry.

They call her CONVERTIBLE TOP: She's been a brunette, a redhead, and a blonde.

They call him COOKIE: He has such a crummy look.

They call him COP: When he meets a girl, he wants to make a pinch.

They call him CORN: In school he was always at the foot of the class.

They call him CORKSCREW: He's so crooked.

They call her CROWBAR: She's not so much to crow about, but she doesn't bar a thing.

They call her CRYSTAL: She's always on the watch, and gives you a glassy stare.

They call him DETECTIVE: Girls say his hands have built-in search warrants.

They call him DON JUAN: The girls "Don Juan" to have anything to do with him.

They call him DRIP: You can hear him, but you can't turn him off.

They call him DRY CLEANER: He's a wolf who works fast and leaves no ring.

They call him EGG: He's too full of himself to hold anything else.

They call him EXCLAMATION POINT: He's always blowing his top.

They call him FIGHTING QUAKER: He quakes more than he fights.

They call him FISH: He gets into trouble because he can't keep his mouth shut.

They call her FLOWER: She's often potted.

They call her FORTUNETELLER: As a gold digger, she can tell a man's fortune.

They call her FRUIT SALAD: She's as slippery as a banana and as sour as a lemon, and when she's squeezed, you get hit in the eye like a grapefruit.

They call him GARBAGE MAN: He has that certain air about him.

They call him GEOMETRY: He's always found in a triangle.

They call him GIRDLE: He's sure been around women.

They call him GOAT: He's always butting in.

They call her HAZEL: She's a real nut.

They call her HOME GIRL: She's not particular whose home.

They call her ICE CREAM: She's sweet but cold.

They call her INSTANT COFFEE: She's easy to make.

They call her IODINE: She's a drug on the market.

They call him LACE: You'll always find him around a skirt.

They call him LEMON SQUEEZER: He always dances with a wallflower.

They call him LIGHTNING: He conducts himself properly.

They call her LILAC: She can lilac anything.

They call her LIVE WIRE: The way she dresses, there isn't much insulation.

They call him LUKE: He's not so hot.

They call him MAGICIAN: He can turn anything into an argument.

They call him MATCH: He loses his head when he gets lit up.

They call him MATHEMATICIAN: He likes to work with figures —females', that is.

They call him M.D.: He's Mentally Deficient.

They call her MELODY: She's real sharp, knocks guys flat, and boy, does she know the score!

They call him MIRACLE WORKER. It's a miracle when he works.

They call him MOTH: He's been found in many closets.

They call her MOTOR MECHANIC: She's always taking off attire.

They call her MUSCLES: She's in every fellow's arms.

They call her MUSICIAN: She's a snob full of airs.

They call him MYTH: He's a myth-fit.

They call her NAPKIN: She's always in some fellow's lap.

They call him NAT: Short for G-N-A-T.

They call him OCEAN: He's all wet.

They call her PEACH: The tighter you squeeze her, the mushier she gets.

They call him PHOTOGRAPHER: When he's with a girl, he puts out the light. The idea is to see what develops.

They call him PIE: He has lots of crust.

They call her PLYMOUTH ROCK: She has a shape like a Plymouth and a head like a rock.

They call him PNEUMATIC DRILL: He's such a bore.

They call her RADIO STATION: Anybody can pick her up, especially late at night.

They call her RESOLUTION: She's hard to keep.

They call him RIVER: The biggest part of him is his mouth.

They call her RUMOR: She goes from mouth to mouth.

They call him SPIDER: He's always living in suspense.

They call him THEORY: He hardly ever works.

They call him TRAVELER: When he takes a girl out, he always tries to touch points of interest.

They call him TRUCK: He always has a load on.

They call her TURKEY: She's stuffed in the right places

They call her WHEATCAKE: She sure is stacked.

They call him WHEELBARROW: He needs to be pushed.

They call him WIGGLE: He wears his hat all the time because he's afraid his wig'll come off.

They call him WINNIE: He has a voice like a horse.

They call him WRESTLER: He's always throwing his weight around.

Squelches

Look, Dr. Jekyll, you're getting under my Hyde.

You've convinced me about reincarnation—now tell me what part of a horse you were in a previous existence.

I can't actually blame you for your ancestors, but I sure must blame them for you.

Let's play Building and Loan. Just get out of the building and leave me alone.

Whatever is eating you must be suffering from indigestion.

There's nothing the matter with you that a nice, first-class funeral couldn't fix.

If Moses had known anyone like you, there would have been another commandment.

You could make a good living hiring yourself out to scare people with the hiccups.

You impress me as the type of person who always wants to save face, so why don't you stop shooting it off?

Excuse me while I go out for a cup of coffee. I have to steady my nerves before I take another look at you.

I'll bet you're the one who goes to libraries just to tear the last chapter out of mystery novels.

You really have an open mind—and a mouth to match.

Look. I'm not going to engage in a battle of wits with you—I never attack anyone who's unarmed.

You make me wish I had a lower IQ so I could enjoy your company.

You know, I'd like to send you a Valentine, but I haven't figured out how to wrap lace around a time bomb.

I'm really pleased to see you're back—particularly after seeing your face.

Tell me, is that your lower lip, or are you wearing a turtleneck sweater?

You've got the sort of face I don't want to remember, but can't forget.

You're something that one only meets in a nightmare.

It isn't simple to figure out what you've got, but whatever it is, take my advice and get rid of it.

I wouldn't fret so much if I were you—after all, we can't all be mentally sound.

I understand you were an infant prodigy. It's too bad you've continued to act like an infant long after you ceased being a prodigy.

Why don't you leave here and go to the zoo? You'll be less conspicuous there.

It's not the ups and downs in life that bother me—it's the jerks like you.

You remind me of some of those new dances—one, two, three, jerk!

I'll bet you're called a big thinker—by people who lisp.

You have a fine personality—but not for a human being.

It's an experience to have someone like you at this party. May I be the very first to shake you by the throat?

You may think you're a gay buck, but you're only two bits.

Why don't you go and get lost somewhere where they have no Found Department?

I haven't decided yet exactly what piece of my mind to give you, but stick around, I've got quite a choice.

It's no use asking you to act like a human being—you don't do imitations.

I hear they're naming a cake after you—a crumb cake with a lot of crust.

A crumb like you should have stayed in bread.

I can't forget the first time I laid eyes on you—and don't think I haven't tried.

I understand when you were a kid your mother sent your picture to Ripley, and it was promptly returned, marked, "I don't believe it!"

I'm just palpitating to know where you've been all my life— and when you're going back there.

Listen, baboon, don't accuse me of making a monkey out of you. Why should *I* take all the credit?

You sure are a squirrel's idea of Utopia.

You're just perfect at any party as an M.C.—a Mental Case.

You couldn't even entertain a doubt.

It's easy to understand why people like you made Oscar Wilde.

You appear to be as happy as if you were in your right mind.

Why don't you pal around with a half-wit so you can have someone to look up to?

I must say you exemplify the spirit of brotherly shove.

I'd like to help you out. Just tell me which way you came in.

On your way out, could I drop you off somewhere—like a nearby bridge?

You've convinced me of the truth of the old proverb, "Distance lends enchantment."

Look, I've got Christmas ties that aren't as loud and useless as you are.

Why don't you go and have your jocular vein cut?

I've known calamities in my lifetime, but never a vocalamity like you.

You may think you're the big cheese at parties, but you only smell like it.

You remind me of a clarinet—a wind instrument.

I'm going to send you a present—as soon as I can figure out how to wrap up a Bronx cheer.

The longer I know you, the more I depreciate you.

There are plenty of manholes in this town, so why did you have to drop in here?

Your Early American features fascinate me—you look like a buffalo.

Anytime you happen to pass my house, I'll appreciate it.

You may be a tonic to your family, but to me you're a pill.